ALLIANCES IN U.S.
FOREIGN POLICY

Studies in Global Security

Alan Ned Sabrosky, Series Editor

ALLIANCES IN U.S. FOREIGN POLICY

ISSUES IN THE QUEST FOR COLLECTIVE DEFENSE

edited by
Alan Ned Sabrosky

Foreword by
Charles F. Doran

Westview Press / Boulder and London

Studies in Global Security

This Westview softcover edition is printed on acid-free paper and bound in softcovers that carry the highest rating of the National Association of State Textbook Administrators, in consultation with the Association of American Publishers and the Book Manufacturers' Institute.

Published in 1988 in the United States of America by Westview Press, Inc.; Frederick A. Praeger, Publisher; 5500 Central Avenue, Boulder, Colorado 80301

Library of Congress Cataloging-in-Publication Data
Alliances in U.S. foreign policy.
  (Studies in global security)
  Includes index.
  1. United States—Foreign relations—1981– .
2. Alliances. 3. North Atlantic Treaty Organization.
I. Sabrosky, Alan Ned. 1941– . II. Title: Alliances
in U.S. foreign policy. III. Series.
E876.A46 1988   327.73   86-4039
ISBN 0-8133-7195-3

Composition for this book originated with conversion of the editor's word-processor disks. This book was produced without formal editing by the publisher.

Printed and bound in the United States of America

The paper used in this publication meets the requirements of the American National Standard for Permanence of Paper for Printed Library Materials Z39.48-1984.

6   5   4   3   2   1

323489

To Julie—
An Ally of Great Value

CONTENTS

FOREWORD: PROBING THE ORIGINS OF CONTEMPORARY ALLIANCE THOUGHT

Charles F. Doran

Analysis contained in these essays requires at the outset twofold comment. First, while policy-oriented and deeply relevant to the on-going debate concerning alliance relations, these essays are informed both by international political theory and by an empirical familiarity with world and U.S. domestic politics. Although the mix varies from essay to essay, the combination of theory and empirical analysis provides a solid historical base for policy generalization. Policy analysis thus springs from more than the last newspaper account of events, while sacrificing nothing in terms of relevancy.

Second, the authors contributing to this volume represent a new generation of mature scholarship in the United States. Neither the Great Depression nor World War II are events with which many of these authors are personally familiar. The European Community, the great postwar alliance systems, and the Cold War are the givens of world politics which they have known personally and which provide background for their analysis, minus an identification with the turbulence that made the "givens" reality. One event, the Vietnam War, is perhaps freshest in their awareness. Assumptions regarding America's wealth are also different from the prior generation of writers who believed that demand-led economics could underpin every defense need. Also, unlike some of the writers in the 1970s who feared too much growth, many of these authors fear that there will be too little. Yet these writers are not so much easily categorized ideologically or in partisan terms, as they are pragmatic and prepared to ask questions requiring answers that go to the premises of alliance thought as much as to tactics or to the manner of implementation.

Thus, in approach to analysis and in terms of personal experience and mindset, these authors represent something new in the discussion of alliance politics. Despite arriving at different conclusions about its impact, these authors are perhaps responding to a common, sometimes implicit theoretical proposition about alliance participation and therefore about the determinants of alliance cohesion. The proposition reads something like this:

> To what extent does participation in an alliance increase foreign policy benefits through enhancing one's own security and through reducing one's own probability of getting involved in war, and to what extent does participation decrease those benefits through entanglement in wars, precipitated by allies, that serve to undermine one's own security and increase one's own frequency or intensity of war involvement?

Alliances are therefore seen as manifesting both collective and non-collective goods. Neither peace nor security is seen as totally indivisible. Or, at the least, peace and security are contributed to unevenly and may, in some cases, provide selective benefits and costs. Greece does not contribute the same amount of resources to NATO as Britain. While each may provide a common defense against Soviet aggression, the differential risk that each will drag other alliance members into third-party conflicts may also be a factor that the other alliance members inevitably will use to condition their own participation.

Even the primary alliance focus involving the Soviet threat may be at issue if an alliance member thinks that it somehow could escape the consequences of attack by opting out of the alliance. Or the primary focus may be at issue if the state feels it is likely to gain less in security terms than it risks in associating with another alliance member that acts precipitously toward the Soviet Union and thus invites a challenge to the alliance as a whole. All of these calculations amount to dangerous thinking as regards alliance health. Moreover, it is only the mutuality and magnitude of external threat that prevent such thought from becoming debilitating for an alliance as a whole.

Historical empirical evidence shows, according to Alan Sabrosky, that when faced with the test of war, most alliance members have tended to stand aside or remain neutral. This is one of the most seminal discoveries in the empirical literature for policy. Along with the free rider effect expounded by Olson and Zeckhouser, it is one of the two most pregnant empirical findings to date concerning alliance behavior. Sabrosky also concludes that the "American system of alliances is now more entangling than it is supportive of American interests" and that NATO is "far more precarious than its advocates would have us believe." He thus urges caution when drawing conclusions about the responsiveness of alliance performance.

In a brilliant assessment of the implications for alliance cohesion of changing deterrent policy and the technical response to those changes, Earl Ravenal is not surprised by the questions raised by Europeans about the credibility of extended deterrence nor by the American shift toward defensive doctrine and the Strategic Defense Initiative. He finds the notion that Americans would sacrifice their cities in an attempt to defend Western Europe from Soviet occupation as problematic, just as he views SDI as an attempt to meet the European demand for a more perfect deterrent that would restore the American edge. But SDI, even if operable in some mode and cost-effective, may create problems of its own with respect to technical stability. His doubts regarding the plausibility of extended deterrence are only compounded by his doubts regarding the continuing American economic capacity to pay disproportionate costs of defense under present alliance terms.

Each of these challenges to traditional alliance thought require a far-reaching rebuttal. Some of the responses to these challenges emerge from the other essays appearing in this volume. For example, James O'Leary asserts that new coproduction arrangements between firms on each side of national boundaries are beginning to surmount protectionist pressures, thus reducing friction between allies. The shift of economic power towards Asia is also beginning to integrate U.S. security policy more closely with some of the NICs and Japan and to obtain from them somewhat larger contributions to their own defense. Likewise, according to Karen McPherson, divergent options within NATO are often more the result of differing domestic priorities among the member nations than of "inherent weakness" in the alliance itself. Gregory Foster maintains that public opinion is the fulcrum of alliance cohesion. While he laments the "gulf" that presently separates public opinion on both sides of the Atlantic and among the European allies themselves, he prescribes the formulation of a NATO public opinion strategy of the sort favored by Grethe Vaerno (Norwegian parliamentary member) stressing public diplomacy and employing propaganda, information, and cultural exchange.

But in one of the most informative essays in the volume, Terry Deibel shows that instead of concentrating on the economic underpinning of alliance relations, the coordination of divergent domestic political priorities among governments, and the effort to influence the opinion of mass publics, the United States since the latter years of the Carter presidency has expanded the scope of America's alliance commitments, especially in the Third World.

Thus we return to the problem noted by Sabrosky at the beginning of the volume, namely that growing obligations through alliance expansion are adding greater alliance burdens without contributing substantially to American security or quite possibly to the security and stability of some of the regions affected by these new arrangements. Similarly, the expansion of alliance commitments does little to solve the problem stressed by Ravenal concerning the resolution of nuclear strategic confidence within NATO on the one hand or concerning the spiraling U.S. Federal and trade deficits on the other.

Still, one wonders whether the strategic predicament of the alliance is quite so devastating as the sharpness of contemporary debate seems to reveal. One wonders also whether escape from economic torment is not possible without destroying the basis for alliance. Finally, one wonders whether the true source of alliance stability does not lie elsewhere than with internal strategic and burden-sharing matters, as it always has.

NATO's strategic predicament has always been latent even when the United States possessed strategic superiority, a condition that disappeared by the late 1960s. The difference is that the predicament is now discussed in the classrooms and in the streets rather than solely among a comparatively small circle of strategic analysts. Ravenal has focussed on one side of the predicament, namely, the possible reluctance of the United States to use strategic nuclear weapons to defend Western Europe from overwhelming attack. The other side of the predicament is that the United States would be too ready, in the eyes of some Europeans, to use theatre nuclear weapons in Europe to stop an overwhelming conventional attack in order to keep the war limited to the European continent. Each side of the predicament existed 20 years ago and exists today, yet NATO persists. Why?

First, nearly a million Americans, servicemen and families, remain in Europe as a guarantee not only that the United States would come to the aid of Europe if under attack but that in doing so the United States would act prudently and expeditiously. The trip-wire notion is as valid today as it ever was.

Second, the third leg of the strategic Triad, Submarine-launched Ballistic Missiles, remains invulnerable to attack and is the key element of second-strike capability. As long as this invulnerability continues, and as long as the American will to defend does not falter if deterrence fails, the Soviet Union would commit suicide by attacking Western Europe. An attack that could not be repelled by conventional means would quickly escalate. Escalation that struck the Soviet homeland, as it surely would, could not be kept European. But a preemptive strategic nuclear exchange, initiated by the Soviet Union against the U.S. land-based targets, would unleash the American second-strike against Soviet cities. In such a total war, American cities would not be spared either. But the logic of vertical and horizontal escalation is clear enough and relentless enough to make a Soviet attack on Western Europe of extremely low probability since it would be suicidal. The Kremlin may be tough and even expansionist. It is not suicidal.

Third, what much contemporary deterrence analysis fails to incorporate is an awareness that not only a balance of means is at stake in strategic discussion but a balance of ends as well. This is not to say that a further drift from nuclear parity to Soviet superiority would be inconsequential for NATO strategic policy. What an introduction of ends into foreign policy discussion entails is a recognition that each foreign policy end has a utility, that this utility varies with the identity of each foreign policy objective, and that the utility of an objective has to be very high (e.g., defense of a close ally or defense of one's own territory) to risk loss of many cities through nuclear exchanges. In practical terms, this means that while Henry IV could say that Paris was well worth a mass, could a modern Kremlin leader say that Paris, albeit a Paris in rubble, is worth the loss of most large Soviet cities? The utility of an attack on Western Europe by Soviet forces facing imminent and large-scale escalation, given the continuing reality of second-strike capability on the part of the United States, plus the not inconsiderable nuclear force available to Britain, France, and China, is simply not high enough to justify an attack.

NATO strategic stability is probably a lot more robust than some accounts of the dilemmas of extended deterrence would seem to make it. No deterrent strategy is perfect or free from the anxiety of practical implementation. Second-strike capability, and a proper military balance as well as an equilibrium of interests and means, continues to be essential. But from this analytic perspective, the continuity of NATO strategic policy remains unbroken.

Ravenal is correct regarding the challenge of burden-sharing. Adjustments must occur and soon. They will not leave the distribution of responsibility and affiliation unaffected. But before concluding that NATO will disappear because of this economic challenge, the analyst ought to consider opportunity costs. What are the alternatives? Western Europe has the economic capability to absorb a larger share of the costs. From its perspective, better to pay more of these costs and retain American forces in Europe and the American nuclear guarantee than to attempt to "go it alone." While this is not the place for an extensive defense of the thesis that economic adjustment is possible and advantageous for Western Europe as well as the United States, the thesis needs an airing.

Finally, in considering alliance cohesion, the key factor as always is the nature of the threat and perception of that threat. The Soviet Union has periodically obliged the NATO allies by saving the alliance through renewal of threat. The invasion of Czechoslovakia in 1968, the occupation of Afghanistan, and the manipulation of Poland during the solidarity crisis all serve to remind attentive Westerners of the Soviet capacity for and style of domination. Ultimately, it is Soviet power and Soviet actions that determine whether NATO remains alive and healthy or whether it follows the fate of CENTO and, to a lesser extent (because of ASEAN), SEATO. So far the Soviet Union has never disappointed the architects of the principal Western alliance system.

This volume thus poses critical questions about alliance purpose and cohesion that demand a response. The essays remind the reader that U.S. resources are finite and that choices must be made concerning the nature and scope of alliance commitments. The authors probe weak points and offer prescriptions for alliance reform. Sober and articulate, these analysts of Western alliance thought address the type of policy discussion that will preoccupy government decisionmakers throughout the coming decade.

PREFACE

Editing any book is always an interesting and instructive experience. This is certainly the case when the subject being examined is of such significance to the United States. No country truly can do well alone in the modern world, whatever its pretensions to the contrary might be. Choosing good partners, managing alliances well, and avoiding or dispensing with entanglements thus can have a major impact on this country's prospects for success in its endeavors abroad. Included in this volume are original papers addressing a selected set of issues that appear to be especially salient with regard to U.S. alliances in general and to NATO—our most important pact—in particular.

Surprises, of course, come about in any editorial exercise. Good contributors, however, help make those surprises pleasant ones, and I have had the great fortune to have such contributors in this instance. All of the people at Westview Press have smoothed my path as well; special thanks are due to Dean Birkenkamp, Susan McEachern, and Lea Leadbeater, whose advice and assistance were particularly valuable. My friends and colleagues at the Army War College provided a congenial working environment, with Janet Smith laboring mightily to transform my chaotic scribblings into a final typescript. To one and all, my gratitude.

Alan Ned Sabrosky
Carlisle Barracks, Pennsylvania

1

ALLIANCES IN
U.S. FOREIGN POLICY

Alan Ned Sabrosky

INTRODUCTION

Scarcely a day passes without some reference to "alliances" or "international partnership" appearing in the media. We are told that the North Atlantic Treaty Organization (NATO) is in difficulty because of divisions within it over trade relationships with the Soviet Union. We hear of commitments which the United States has undertaken to safeguard the security of Israel. We recall the uncertainty that appeared in Washington as the South Atlantic War of 1982 pitted two allies, Great Britain and Argentina, against one another over the Falklands (or Malvinas, as the Argentines called them). We may reflect upon various assertions that the United States remains a reliable guarantor of the security of its partners, despite certain misadventures in Southeast Asia in the past decade. And we may view with either chagrin or satisfaction (depending on our politics and the issue at hand) the U.S. Government's decision to forego concluding a formal alliance with South Africa, to speak of Saudi Arabia as an ally, and to warn that the fall of the pro-American government in El Salvador may threaten other U.S. allies in Central America.

What is all too often lost in such considerations, however, is a full understanding of both the diverse character of alliance relationships in the modern world, and the proper role of alliances in U.S. foreign policy. All alliances are not created equal. They do not endow their members with the same degree of safety or influence in world politics, however convenient it may be in some circles to present alliances in such an oversimplified way for public consumption. And they do not play an equally obvious or important role in U.S. foreign policy,

1

however comfortable we may have become with their presence since the end of the Second World War.

The object of this paper is to bring an added measure of clarity to our understanding of America's alliances in the contemporary international order. This will be done in four steps. *First*, I will discuss the concept of alliance in a general sense. *Second*, the U.S. experience with alliances will be appraised. *Third*, I will briefly examine one of this country's most current foreign commitments—NATO—in light of that experience. *Fourth*, and finally, I will outline the preferred role alliances should play in the years ahead, and how this country might best move in that direction, in order to provide a framework upon which the following chapters may build.

ALLIANCES IN WORLD POLITICS

Consensus on anything is rare in world politics. Few, however, disagree with the contention that alliances traditionally have been seen as one of the essential elements of any balance of power system. Within that context, alliances may be seen as a "resource" which nations seek to use to achieve certain objectives.[1] One such objective is to augment implicitly the *power* a state may bring to the game of nations, giving it more political leverage during peacetime than it would be able to provide for itself alone at the same cost and risk. Another objective is to enhance the *stability* of the relevant international system by using an alliance either to deter a potential adversary or to restrain a rambunctious associate. And a third national objective is to have a *wartime partner*, augmenting its own capabilities and avoiding a "worst case" outcome of having to fight alone. In all instances, of course, the controlling principle is theoretically straightforward: *an alliance must enhance a nation's security, or at least not undermine it.*

A number of factors influence the extent to which an alliance actually gives a nation the potential to attain the aforementioned objectives in accordance with that general principle. These include a nation's position in the international hierarchy and the distribution of effective power in the world; variations in its definition of national interests and foreign policy goals; and the quality of its leadership, as well as the efficiency of its governmental decisionmaking apparatus. These, and similar, considerations necessarily enter into any assessment of the degree to which alliances in general, or a specific alliance in particular, may actually live up to the expectations of its signatories.

Looking at the domestic and international political context within which alliances must operate, while necessary, is obviously not sufficient. One must also look at the alliances themselves. Alliances may truly be considered "many-splendored things," at least in the sense that each alliance incorporates some combination of a number of specific attributes. One is the *type of bond* that defines an alliance commitment.[2] A "formal" or *de jure* bond exists when all of the participants (described in some instances as "high contracting parties") have ratified the agreement in accordance with their respective constitutional or statutory procedures. This creates a mutual (and supposedly binding) commitment recognizable under international law. An "informal" bond reflects an *apparent* or *de facto* commitment on behalf of one party that may or may not be reciprocated by the object of that commitment. Such a bond may be created by executive agreement; it may occur in the context of (e.g.) a series of arms sales or grants; it can arise as an adjunct to a formal alliance which specifies still other countries as "protocol states," protected by the alliance but not obligated to endorse it; or it can obtain in conjunction with a foreign policy doctrine that extended a protective "security umbrella" over some part of the world. The extent to which such informal pacts are considered binding in any sense of the term obviously depends upon the precise combination of circumstances operative in each case.

A second attribute is the *membership of the alliance.* There are actually two aspects to this attribute: (a) the *size* of the membership, and (b) the *power status* of the signatories.[3] In the former case, one speaks of a distinction between "bilateral" alliances (of only two states), and "multilateral" alliances (with three or more states). In the latter instance, the classic distinction is between "major" powers on the one hand, and "minor" powers on the other. Today, a third category—that of "middle" powers (e.g., France and Japan)—is being used with increasing frequency to take account of the more complex character of power and influence relationships that obtains in the modern world.

A third attribute is the *class* of an alliance commitment. This represents the type of obligation nominally assumed by the signatories to a pact. There are a number of different ways of categorizing alliances in this respect. One commonly used procedure differentiates among: (a) *offensive* or *wartime* alliances, in which the signatories band together for the express purpose of waging war against some third party; (b) *defensive* or *mutual security* pacts, in which the signatories agree to come to one another's assistance in the event a member of the alliance is attacked; (c) *neutrality* or *nonaggression* pacts, whose members agree not to become involved in a war *against* one another; and (d) what is called an *entente*, which is an "understanding" that can range from a *de facto* offensive/defensive pact to an expression of mutual interest in one another's well-being (many informal pacts would necessarily fall into this category).

The fourth and final attribute is the *scope* of the accord. This involves considerations of: (a) the formal *duration* of the pact, including the provisions, if any, for renewal; (b) the various *obligations* or *burden-sharing arrangements* undertaken by the signatories on their collective behalf; (c) the *casus foederis*—that is, the conditions under which the alliance commitments assumed by the signatories will be activated; and (d) the *decisionmaking process* involved in preparing for, or responding to, the contingencies the alliance was designed to meet. The precise scope of an alliance is often extremely sensitive, since it may entail the identification of specific adversaries and specific national objectives that the signatories do not want to become public knowledge. Thus, the public or "open" document defining a pact may be couched in somewhat ambiguous or overly general terms, with those provisions requiring more delicate handling being reserved for secret protocols or informal "memoranda of understanding" among the alliance partners.

In all cases, of course, one must be careful not to ascribe undue significance to the formal terms of a pact. It is always necessary to distinguish the *actual* character of an alliance relationship from the *nominal* one contained in the accord itself. World politics and national interests change, and with them the nature of whatever bond might exist between two or more nations. A nominally weak alliance may become stronger in practice over time, even if its "official" character does not change, as in the case of the Anglo-French *Entente Cordiale* of 1904. On the other hand, putatively binding obligations, such as that which aligned Italy with Germany and Austria-Hungary in the pre-World War I "Triple Alliance," may turn out to be worthless when put to the test.[4] Formal allies may even attack one another, a fact demonstrated most strikingly when Germany violated its nonaggression pact with the Soviet Union in 1941. There is also some question with regard to the role alliances play in achieving the objectives set out for them. Credible alliances may well lubricate the balance-of-power mechanism in world politics and avert some wars, but it is difficult to demonstrate either point empirically in a conclusive manner. It is equally difficult to refute persuasively contentions that truly binding alliances may actually reduce a nation's diplomatic freedom of action in peacetime, and encourage the expansion of what might have been a more limited conflict if war occurs. At best, the evidence is mixed in each instance.

These caveats notwithstanding, certain empirical regularities or patterns of performance do appear to exist in the historical record of alliances over the past two centuries.[5] Perhaps the most intriguing conclusion to be drawn from that record is that alliances have not performed nearly so well as the conventional wisdom would have it,

TABLE 1.1

THE WAR PERFORMANCE OF ALLIANCE PARTNERS,
1816-1965

War Performance[c]

Time Period	Fights Alongside (Honors)		Remains Neutral (Abstains)		Fights Against (Violates)		Total	
	N	%	N	%	N	%	N	%
1816-1899	12	32%[a] (7)[b]	25	65% (14)	1	3% (1)	38	100% (22)
1900-1965	36	26 (20)	83	60 (47)	20	14 (11)	139	100 (78)
1900- 1945	31	27 (18)	64	56 (36)	19	17 (11)	114	100 (65)
1946- 1965	5	20 (3)	19	76 (11)	1	4 (1)	25	100 (15)
1816-1965	48	(27)%	108	(61)%	21	(12)%	177	(100)%

[a]Percentage of row (time period) total.
[b]Percentage of all war-performance opportunities (N=177).
[c]A "war performance opportunity" occurs when a nation with an active formal alliance becomes involved in a war, thus activating the casus foederis.

SOURCE: Alan Ned Sabrosky, "Interstate Alliances: Their Reliability and the Expansion of War," in J. David Singer (ed.), The Correlates of War: II (New York: The Free Press, 1980), p. 177.

at least with regard to the fundamental "fight-the-war" function of reliably binding states to come to one another's assistance in war. As Table 1.1 demonstrates, the most common response of alliance partners when their pacts were put to the test of war was to stand aside and remain neutral. Such behavior could hardly be reassuring to states which believed alliances did represent an added measure of security in war.

To be sure, there are some indications that nations in alliances are more inclined to fight alongside one another than is the case in the absence of such commitments. Some alliances, in some eras, also do better than others in this respect. In general, the most reliable alliances (in the "fight-the-war" sense used above) over time have tended to be formal bilateral defense pacts composed of states of equivalent power status, with reasonably well-crafted limitations on the scope of the commitments assumed by the alliance partners. On the other hand, large alliances encompassing states of greatly disparate power that have accepted a broad or open-ended commitment within the alliance, or neutrality and nonaggression pacts of any type, have had a much more checkered past. In an alliance, in short, it seems that diversity and ambiguity are often incompatible with that reliability of performance during wartime that should be the principal test of the worth of an alliance. It seems that there is much to be said for David Fromkin's remark that "Treaties of alliance are overvalued,"[6] except, perhaps, in a symbolic sense.

NO ENTANGLING ALLIANCES?
THE AMERICAN EXPERIENCE[7]

This admixture of substantive value and symbolic attachment has been an inherent part in the American experience with alliances, once the United States decided to put aside its long-standing determination to avoid "entangling alliances." Indeed, it is well worth remembering that alliance politics are a relatively new experience for this country. Until the Second World War, the United States simply avoided formal alliances to the point that its entry into the First World War in 1917 saw Washington proclaiming America's status as an *associated* power free of the obligations and commitments that presumably tied the *allied* powers to one another. Nor was there anything especially remarkable in the U.S. approach to alliances up to that point. In fact, the United States simply followed a slightly stricter variant of the path taken by Great Britain during the 19th century, recognizing that the absence of formal alliances provided an added degree of diplomatic maneuverability without compromising a security predicated on geography and the limited threat posed by the strategic technology of the era.

All of that changed with the Second World War and the Soviet-American "Cold War" that ensued. Except for the Cold War, it is likely that the United States would have once again foresworn formal military alliances as it had after the First World War, relying on its participation as a leading member of the United Nations to avert the situation that arose in part because of Washington's abstention from the League of Nations. But the onset of the protracted conflict with the Soviet Union made security commitments other than those of the United Nations necessary, while the globalization of the Cold War and the doctrine of containment that accompanied the Communist victory in China (1949) and the armed clashes in Korea (1950–53) and Indochina (1946–54) brought with them a globalization of America's security commitments. Throwing aside its earlier disdain for alliances, the United States entered into the quest for alliances with abandon, structuring an extensive system of formal and informal alliances over the next decade. Prominent multilateral pacts included the Rio Pact (1947), which brought together the nations of the Western Hemisphere; the North Atlantic Treaty Organization, or NATO (1949), which aimed at containing the USSR in Europe; ANZUS (1952), that tied Australia, New Zealand, and the United States to one another; and the Southeast Asia Treaty Organization, or SEATO (1955), organized in response to the Communist victory in Indochina in 1954 and including under its wing the so-called "protocol states" of South Vietnam, Laos, and Cambodia. Bilateral pacts were forged with South Korea, Taiwan (then known as the Republic of China), the Philippines (which was also a member of SEATO), and Japan. And informal arrangements abounded, ranging from the U.S. role as a "silent partner" in the Central Treaty Organization (CENTO) and its avowed commitment to the security of Israel, to American endorsement of various Third World regimes via the medium of security and economic assistance programs. Even the level of "detente" with the Soviet Union espoused in the early 1970s and reflected in the Soviet-American "Declaration of Basic Principles" (1972) represented a *de facto* nonaggression pact that, in time, might have evolved into an entente with interesting implications for other alliance systems.[8]

By the mid-1950s, an imposing edifice was in place. The nation which had once declared its intention of staying outside of the balance of power system with its network of alliances found itself at the center of the most extensive system of alliances in the world. More to the point, that system had much to show for its existence, at least in its early years. Western Europe remained outside of the Soviet orbit; containment largely worked; and alliance partners (or at least some of them) did band together on occasion, even if somewhat belatedly as in the case of the Dominican Republic crisis of 1965. But subsequent events have raised a number of disturbing questions about the substantive worth of that alliance system to the United States. Prominent among these events have been the demise of the three Indochinese protocol states in 1975, presaging the demise of SEATO a few years later; the disappearance of CENTO from the contemporary diplomatic lexicon; and the compounding of injury with insult when the United States, in its quest for improved diplomatic relations with the People's Republic of China (PRC), accepted the PRC's position on Taiwan and unilaterally abrogated its defense pact with that country.[9] Less terminal, but no less injurious to the reputation of America's alliance system, have been the continuing uneasiness within NATO on a variety of issues affecting the alliance, and the acrimonious exchanges with Israel.

Although it is possible to exaggerate the individual importance of any of these developments, their combined impact adds credence to the position that the edifice of the U.S. alliance system is considerably more impressive than its substance, given its presumably controlling objectives of adding to, or at least not detracting from, American security and the safeguarding of American interests. On balance, it is difficult to escape the conclusion that the American system of alliances is now more entangling than it is supportive of American interests, and that the United States has come to find itself in the company of relatively few genuine allies, many clients, and several obvious encumbrances.

There are three principal reasons why this situation has come to pass. They are: (a) *overcommitment*, (b) *miscommitment*, and (c) *mismanagement*. In the first instance, the United States simply undertook more security commitments than either it or its more active alliance partners possessed the resources to defend if threatened. The resulting overextension produced the mismatch of capabilities and commitments so evident in the existence of multiple contingencies drawing on the same forces, and contributed to the creation of a strategic vacuum in which the United States finds itself today with no national strategy that persuasively links ends and means. In the second place, the United States associated itself with a number of unsavory regimes whose only claim on the United States was a nominal anti-Communism that they espoused in order to obtain American support. That association placed the United States in the uncomfortable position of being unwilling to enforce change in nominal allies when they were not directly threatened for fear of losing influence, and unable to support such states when they were threatened if that required a protracted and costly American commitment on their behalf.[10] And finally, the United States undertook a series of asymmetrical arrangements in which reciprocity from the protected alliance partner was all too often lacking, while the decisionmaking process in the larger alliances gave the weaker members of the pact a disproportionate voice in the management of the alliance. Some tension of this type may be inevitable in alliances involving partners of unequal strength, as it places the principles of *sovereign equality* (giving each alliance partner an equal voice in decisions) and *proportionality of power* (in which influence over alliance decisions corresponds to the resources each alliance partner brings with it) in direct conflict with one another. Inevitable or not, however, it has tended to work to the disadvantage of the United States.

It would certainly be unwarranted to assume that all of America's alliances are fatally flawed. But it would be equally unwarranted to assume that the United States could safely ignore the problems described above. A detailed consideration of any U.S. alliance, much less the entire system of alliances, clearly exceeds the scope of this chapter. Nevertheless, the basic character of the U.S. dilemma may be ascertained from an assessment of NATO, a formal multilateral alliance that is America's most important formal foreign commitment.

NATO: A PACT IN PERIL?

In many respects, NATO is a venerable institution, the contemporary analogue of the pre-1914 Habsburg empire. We have become accustomed to its existence, and we have more than a little difficulty contemplating a security environment in which it did not exist.[11] That fact alone may account for the continuing juxtaposition of publicly expressed official optimism about NATO, coupled with frequent reaffirmations of NATO's enduring importance to the West, on the one hand, against private expressions of concern or outright pessimism on the other.

To understand the state of NATO today, it is important to recognize that a combination of Soviet threat, European weakness, and American ambivalence set the stage for NATO, whose importance to both the United States and Western Europe was undeniable. For the United States, NATO became this country's most significant and most powerful overseas commitment—the classic "Cold War" coalition that has persisted independent of the vicissitudes of Soviet-American (or, more broadly put, East-West) relations. It institutionalized the "Europe First" inclination in American foreign policy which had effectively been formalized by the Truman Doctrine of 1947. NATO became the front line of the original doctrine of containment of the Soviet Union, with Western Europe being a *de facto* buffer zone within whose boundaries the opening stages of an East-West war might be fought, and—from an American point of view—hopefully localized. For Western Europe, NATO provided the shield behind which the economic recovery of the ravaged nations of the continent could proceed, and European institutions such as the EEC and the European Parliament could develop. It staved off the extension of Soviet control into Western Europe. It provided a mechanism for the reintegration of West Germany into the European community of nations in much less time than anyone contemplating the devastation wrought by the Second World War might have thought possible. And, perhaps of greatest importance, its tenure has been associated with peace in Europe for nearly four decades—

something that Europeans of an earlier generation could only have contemplated with envy.[12]

The relative importance ascribed to these considerations has varied over time, as well as across the membership of NATO. Throughout, however, there has been the acknowledgment (formal or informal) that NATO as an institution rested on four pillars, *all* of which were seen to be essential to its continuation as a viable organization. These were:

- A common perception of a threat posed by the Soviet Union as a great power with expansionist tendencies, reinforced in the eyes of some (but not all) NATO members by concern with Communism as an ideology, that could only be countered by the Western nations acting in concert.
- The recognition that stability and security in Europe, and thus in the West in general, could only be preserved by the maintenance of a "balance of imbalances" in which Soviet conventional (or "theater") superiority in Europe would be offset by an American security guarantee based on the possession by the United States of a credible nuclear *advantage* over the USSR that was meaningful in both a political and (less dramatically) military sense.
- The development in short order of economic cooperation between the United States and Western Europe in the context of European economic recovery and the creation of robust domestic economies capable of meeting the demands of NATO as well as the requirements of their domestic programs.
- The existence of convergent, or at least not overtly conflictful, interests among the members of NATO within the alliance, as well as shared or parallel goals outside of the geographical parameters of NATO, especially with regard to Soviet actions in the Third World (recognizing that the behavior of the USSR in the Third World would not automatically strike all members of NATO as being as much of a concern as the same Soviet action in the vicinity of Europe itself).

An appraisal of the state of NATO today is far from reassuring when seen in the light of the aforementioned pillars of the alliance. Much, of course, *has* been done well, and the fact that NATO has persevered despite past challenges to its integrity (e.g., the stillborn notion of a European Defense Community, the combined crises of Suez and Hungary in 1956, the debate over the Multilateral Force in the early 1960s, and the withdrawal of France from the integrated military structure of the alliance in 1967) says much about its durability under stress.

On the other hand, to acknowledge what has been accomplished without noting changes that have taken place to NATO's disadvantage in the intervening years would only add to the official image so often presented to the public eye. NATO's current assets are clearly impressive, but—those assets notwithstanding—its current state is far more precarious than its advocates would have us believe. Put directly, none of the four pillars of NATO discussed above remains intact today in its original form, if at all, or commands widespread acceptance. Manifestations of this development abound. One need reflect upon only such events as the divergent reactions within NATO to the Soviet invasion of Afghanistan and the unrest in Poland; the seemingly interminable debate on the equity of burden-sharing within the alliance; the divisive debate over the deployment of intermediate range nuclear forces in accordance with the NATO decision of December 1979; and the conflicting arguments over the relative strategic importance of domestic economic interests that appeared in the United States (over the lifting of the grain embargo against the USSR) and in Western Europe (over the natural gas pipeline to be constructed with the Soviet Union), to understand that such numerous symptoms suggest that all is far from well with NATO.

Why this should be the case in an alliance whose intrinsic merit has been assumed by so many for so long provides a case study in the politics of misalliance. Its importance to both the United States and to Western Europe notwithstanding, a concatenation of *military*, *economic*, *political*, and *institutional* developments have gravely weakened the substantive (if not the symbolic) value of NATO as a reliable mechanism for the safeguarding of U.S. interests and the exercise of American influence.[13]

From a *military* perspective, the crucial consideration is not simply the undeniable growth in Soviet conventional capabilities in the European theater of operations, or even the failure of arms control negotiations to check the Soviet military buildup. The Soviet Union has always had an advantage in aggregate conventional military power in the NATO–Warsaw Pact balance, and its sustained buildup over the past two decades has increased the extent of that advantage rather than the fact that it existed. Moreover, since any arms control agreement acceptable to the West (i.e., an agreement that would produce verifiable parity at lower force levels than now exist) would require the USSR to give up a prevailing advantage that it considers important for the exercise of influence abroad, it is not surprising that the only arms control agreement (broadly defined) in Europe has been the Helsinki Treaty of 1975, a *de facto* "confidence building measure" (CBM) which arguably give the USSR far more than it conceded to the West. The central issue is that the nuclear advantage that gave NATO a measure of escalatory advantage over the USSR passed out of existence as a matter of policy, begun by former Defense Secretary Robert McNamara during the Kennedy Administration and continued during the SALT process. It may be, in objective terms, that escalatory dominance embodied in a nuclear NATO advantage has not been an essential component of deterrence in Europe. But the perception exists that it was essential, and the uncertainty over the reliability of the United States and the adequacy of linkage between NATO theater forces and the American strategic deterrent has arisen as that nuclear advantage has waned.

Coupled with that military consideration has been a series of *economic* developments that have made the United States and its principal Western European NATO partners economic competitors at the same time as they have been military partners and political associates. The varying degrees of robustness of the various national economies, plus the sense of unease associated with living at the end of a precarious energy lifeline that pervades most of NATO Europe, contributes to differences in economic security within the alliance. NATO Europe has also had greater interest in economic exchanges with the Soviet Union and its Eastern European clients than has been the case with the United States, both because of simple geographical proximity and as a function of a less restrictive approach on issues of East-West trade taken by most Western European governments than would be preferred in the United States today. And finally, the European predisposition to allocate more resources to a variety of social welfare programs than to defense, relative to the practice in the United States, has given rise to a debate over the proper allocation of "burden-sharing" within the alliance. Indeed, the uneven execution of the so-called "3% Solution" of 1977, wherein NATO members agreed in principle to allocate sufficient resources to defense to produce a 3 percent real annual increase in defense outlays, is both illustrative of the different economic priorities that obtain within NATO and indicative of the economic divisions within the alliance.

The *political* problems within NATO are both reflections of the military and economic issues noted above, and divisive factors in their own right. A crucial issue is the misunderstanding of detente that has prevailed for more than a decade, especially in Western Europe. Too many have advocated both detente and arms control (the latter as presumed evidence of either the fact or the progress of detente) as ends worth having on their own terms, rather than as possible means of enhancing national and alliance security. This, of course, is a mistake the Soviet Union has not made. But the preoccupation with detente in most of Western Europe, and the occasional quest for detente in the United States, has divided NATO and inhibited enhancing NATO's defense posture. In addition, sharp and growing divisions exist over a variety of so-called "out of area" issues, principally the Middle East, Southwest Asia, and Central America. Put briefly, the U.S. support for Israel, preparations for intervention in Southwest Asia in certain contingencies (highlighted by the institutionalization of the original "rapid deployment force" in the U.S. Central Command), and adamant opposition to Communist-supported insurgencies in Central America run counter to the predominant (but not unanimous) European support for Palestinian self-determination, reluctance to countenance out-of-area military interventions within the context of the NATO charter, and disenchantment with many of the regimes buttressed by the United States in Central America. And here, the relative merits of the contending positions are less important than the fact that their contentiousness weakens NATO cohesion. Finally, it does not help NATO that three of its principal members are viewed with unease by many other members of the alliance. France, albeit no longer part of the military structure of NATO, is sufficiently a part of the Atlantic Alliance that its predisposition to act in an independent and frequently contrary fashion produces almost as much uncertainty within NATO as it must within Soviet councils, to the detriment of effective NATO operational planning. The Federal Republic of Germany, although a staunch member of the alliance that is fully committed to democracy, still labors under the burden of what Germans often call the "historical circumstances" that are the legacy of World War II, restricted both by NATO decisions and its own self-doubt from being as active a member of the alliance as it ought to be. And the United States has simply not demonstrated in recent years the ability to lead the alliance in a confident, informed and decisive manner, contributing to uncertainty in NATO about American steadfastness that cannot but weaken the alliance.

The *institutional* problems, in the final analysis, are perhaps the most significant, since many of the preceding problems are a function of national policies and governmental styles of leadership that are potentially amenable to change. The basic institutional edifice of NATO, however, cannot be altered appreciably without altering at the same time the fundamental character of the alliance, and perhaps dismantling it. One such problem is the fact that NATO decisions have all too often come to be based on a least common denominator of consensus to produce an outcome acceptable to all. Given the sharply different capabilities, foreign policy positions, and perceptions of threat that exist within the alliance, that least common denominator can be so low that a member of the alliance may do nothing at all without violating at least the spirit of the decision. The fate of the "3% Solution" mentioned earlier is a case in point. A second problem is that the larger members of the alliance, whose participation essentially determines whether or not NATO would have a chance to prevail if the *casus foederis* came to be invoked, are frequently hamstrung by the weaker members of the alliance, some of whom seem dedicated to the proposition that they are in the alliance to obtain as much security at as little cost to themselves and as much risk to others as possible. The 1979 decision of some NATO members to support the deployment of Intermediate Range Nuclear Forces (INF), as long as they were based elsewhere so that others would incur whatever risks attended that deployment, and to make even that commitment hostage to Soviet behavior,[14] reflects both this problem area and the preceding one.

In sum, NATO has become something of a paradox. Some form of a security arrangement in Western Europe is undoubtedly necessary for the United States, given the consequences for American interests of the "finlandization" or absorption of most or all of Western Europe by the Soviet Union. What is not apparent is the long-term ability of NATO to serve that function. The years ahead are going to be even more demanding than those of the 1970s, and the problems that have beset NATO in the 1970s and early 1980s are unlikely to become less troublesome. The United States needs to acknowledge that its NATO allies possess both interests and vulnerabilities that are different from those of the United States; it must be more sensitive to the different political currents that prevail among such different states; and it must avoid sending conflicting signals to its allies, as occurred when the United States sequentially lifted the grain embargo on the USSR and then opposed the European decision to construct a natural gas pipeline in conjunction with the USSR. Europeans, for their part, need to dispense with the habit of criticizing the United States regardless of what the United States does; they must understand that reciprocity is essential, and that they cannot indefinitely demand U.S. assistance in Europe without assisting the United States actively outside of Europe; and they need to make greater efforts in Europe in their own defense than they have done in the past. Whether these things can be accomplished within the context of NATO as it is currently structured and managed, however, is far from certain, and Americans should understand fully the consequences likely to obtain if NATO proves unable to meet that challenge.

THE FUTURE OF AMERICA'S ALLIANCES

The preceding discussion of U.S. alliance commitments, with specific reference to NATO, highlights the dilemma with which the United States must come to terms. The United States clearly needs good allies in the modern world; "America alone" has ceased to be a feasible option. On the other hand, the alliances the United States does have, on balance, seem to have become "entangling" in Washington's original use of the term. This is not to attribute any malevolence to America's alliance partners, either in the case discussed in this chapter or in those other pacts not examined here. Most nations do act in accordance with their national interest, or at least seem less vulnerable than the United States to making significant policy commitments on the basis of an ephemeral "moral obligation" or the predisposition of domestic lobbies whose appreciation of the national interest does not seem to be a controlling concern. That the United States does seem to act in such a fashion, and does seem to be vulnerable in that way, says more about the United States than it does about the nations with which the United States has entered into formal or informal alliance commitments. It also lends weight to the argument that "alliances did not entangle us; either life itself did it, or we did it to ourselves."[15]

What, then, ought the United States do about this situation? There is admittedly relatively little that the United States can do about some of its informal commitments. The absence of a formal commitment means that there is nothing to abrogate, and the existence of strong domestic constituencies in support of some of them makes corrective action difficult. In the case of the informal yet apparently binding tie with Israel, for instance, it is difficult to see what might precipitate a final breach in Israeli-U.S. relations if a deliberate Israeli attack upon an American naval vessel, the *de facto* dispersal or disenfranchisement of the Palestinians and the invasion of a neighboring Lebanon have not sufficed to bring that about. Perhaps all that can be done in such instances is to limit the damage such commitments cause by working as extensively as possible with other regional states, either directly or through the good offices of third parties.

More, however, can be done with formal commitments. Let me begin by observing that the United States does not need any more formal alliance commitments, especially multilateral ones, that involve states with which the United States does not now have a formal alliance. Let me further observe that the existing system of alliances needs to be subjected to the closest scrutiny in order to distinguish allies from clients, and to separate encumbrances from them both. In all instances, the objective should be to clarify commitments, build in formal reciprocity, and try to bring America's obligations more into harmony with American capabilities and American interests. This does not mean that the United States should unilaterally abrogate any other bilateral pacts, or withdraw from multilateral alliances. Whatever their objective value to the United States, the image of a United States formally disengaging from still other formal alliance partners could not contribute to international stability or the furtherance of American interests. But specific bilateral pacts can be forged within the parameters of existing multilateral alliances, as was often done by other countries in the past, with the large alliance representing an expression of a general political interest and the bilateral pacts being the operative military alliances. Thus, the United States might retain both NATO and the Rio Pact as regional equivalents of the UN General Assembly, useful for debate but not much else. But it would structure bilateral arrangements with (e.g.) Great Britain, the Federal Republic of Germany, Italy, and perhaps France on the one hand, and with Brazil on the other, to link the United States with principal regional powers more capable of acting in concert with the United States on matters of mutual interest. And these new pacts should be carefully crafted in accordance with the principles of specificity and reciprocity noted earlier, paying particular attention to limiting the scope of the commitment in keeping with the interests and issues involved. In this way, America may find itself with enough good alliances that are not entangling to permit it to navigate safely in the years ahead. The chapters that follow elaborate upon these and other issues in American alliance politics and their implications for the future.

NOTES

This is an abridged version of a chapter in *Power, Principle and Interests*, edited by J. Salmon, J. P. O'Leary and R. Shultz (Lexington, MA: Ginn Press, 1985). Copyright 1985 by Alan Ned Sabrosky. It was prepared before the author assumed his current position; the views expressed here are the author's own and do not necessarily reflect those of the U.S. Government or any of its agencies.

1. For general discussions of alliances in international relations from differing points of view, see R. E. Osgood, *Alliances and American Foreign Policy* (Baltimore: Johns Hopkins University Press, 1968); George Liska, *Nations in Alliance* (Baltimore: Johns Hopkins University Press, 1968); and O. R. Holsti, P. T. Hopmann, and J. D. Sullivan, *Unity and Disintegration in International Alliances* (New York: Wiley-Interscience, 1973).

2. David Fromkin, "Entangling Alliances," *Foreign Affairs*, 48 (July 1970); B. D. Berkowitz and B. B. de Mesquita, "The Limits of American Foreign Commitments," *Comparative Strategy*, 3/3 (1983); and J. D. Singer and M.

Small, "Formal Alliances, 1815–1939: A Quantitative Description," *Journal of Peace Research*, 3 (January 1966).

3. Singer and Small, "Formal Alliances."

4. Italy chose to remain neutral until 1915, perhaps because it had conflicting alliances with several of the principal warring states in Europe. Its subsequent intervention against Germany and Austria-Hungary in that year represented simultaneously its violation of alliances with those states, and its honoring of alliances with France and Russia.

5. See my "Interstate Alliances: Their Reliability and the Expansion of War," in J. D. Singer (ed.), *The Correlates of War: II* (New York: Free Press, 1980).

6. Fromkin, "Entangling Alliances," p. 689.

7. This discussion draws heavily on my "Allies, Clients and Encumbrances," *International Security Review*, 5/2 (Summer 1980).

8. Richard Rosecrance, "Detente or Entente?," *Foreign Affairs* (1975). It is worth noting that in the heyday of detente, both France and the PRC spoke frequently of "a temptation to condominium" or "parallel hegemonism" as a likely outcome of increasingly close Soviet-American relations.

9. Subsequent Congressional reaffirmation of a continuing U.S. interest in the security of Taiwan does not alter the political signal sent by the unilateral abrogation of the alliance with Taiwan by the United States.

10. The U.S. effort to aid Vietnam is the obvious example of this, but ongoing criticism of U.S. ties to (e.g.) South Korea, the Philippines, and various Latin American regimes also comes to mind.

11. A critical view of NATO is Earl Ravenal, *NATO's Unremarked Demise* (Berkeley: University of California Institute of International Studies, Policy Paper 10, 1979). More supportive of alliances in general, and NATO in particular, is Kenneth Adelman, "Revitalizing Alliances," in W. Scott Thompson (ed.), *National Security in the 1980s: From Weakness to Strength* (San Francisco: Institute for Contemporary Studies, 1980).

12. The obvious exceptions to a respectable era of European peace (if not complete amity!) are the conflict between Greece and Turkey over Cyprus and the minor "cod war" between Great Britain and Iceland, plus internal conflicts such as that in Northern Ireland.

13. See my "NATO: A House Divided?," *Atlantic Quarterly* (Summer 1984) for a discussion of this alliance.

14. This entailed making deployment contingent on the absence of an arms control agreement, or (informally in the view of some signatories) even the absence of promising negotiations with the USSR.

15. Fromkin, "Entangling Alliances," p. 700.

2

EXTENDED DETERRENCE AND ALLIANCE COHESION

Earl C. Ravenal

The parameters of the nuclear age—the diffusion of nuclear weapons and the parity of superpower holdings—have altered the proprieties of national strategy and the political economy of alliance, and thus the shape and dynamics of the international system. In particular, American safety and the extension of American protection to allies are no longer compatible; indeed, in essential aspects they are contradictory. The American guarantee to Europe, expressed in NATO, is correspondingly debilitated. In turn, the bipolar features of the international system have already changed.

The achievement of strategic stability—which is at once the minimum condition for national safety and the maximum condition of safety that is attainable—is a matter that presumes, but also transcends, the "correct" design of nuclear forces and doctrines. Insofar as it involves the broader objective of war-avoidance and the possibility of compartmentalizing conflicts among nations, it invokes the structure of the international system, in two directions: (1) the kind of international system affects the prospects for arms control and a stable nuclear balance; and (2) the degree of strategic stability and the distribution of nuclear arms affect—and in a sense define—the kind of international system. The achievement of elemental safety for a nation, particularly a present alliance guarantor, may require a renunciation of its function of extended deterrence. In turn, if an essential member of the international system were to change this central relationship to allies and antagonists, the international system would necessarily—virtually by definition—change to a looser, more unaligned, structure.

COUPLING AND DECOUPLING

Thirty-six years after the foundation of NATO, the defense of Western Europe still rests on the proposition that an American president will invite the destruction of our cities and the incineration of 100 million of our citizens to repel a Soviet incursion or resist a Soviet ultimatum in Western Europe. On its face, America's war plan—never denied by any president from Truman to Reagan, or by any Secretary of State from George Marshall to George Shultz—is the first use of nuclear weapons, if necessary, to defend Europe. But, under the surface, America's nuclear commitment to Europe is not so sure. The word that encapsulates the problem is "coupling," a term of art used by strategic analysts to connote the integrity of the chain of escalation, from conventional war in Europe to theater nuclear weapons to the final use of America's ultimate strategic weapon.

In a larger sense, coupling connotes the identity of the fates of the peoples, societies, and political systems on both sides of the Atlantic. The root of the problem is that America, the alliance guarantor, hoping to escape the destruction of nuclear war, will seek to put time between the outbreak of war in Europe and the decision to escalate to nuclear weapons, and will take whatever advantage it can of its distance from Europe. Not that an adversary is likely to test American will with an attack on Europe. Odds of, say, 65 percent of an American nuclear response will restrain a potential aggressor. (Even a whiff of American nuclear retaliation is probably enough to keep the Soviet Union from invading Western Europe.) But those odds will not convince allies of their protection. And the real efficacy of extended deterrence is in keeping allies, not just deterring adversaries. There is a nagging asymmetry about nuclear protection: It takes more credibility to keep an ally than to deter an adversary.

Military alliance is an act that cuts two ways: In the obvious sense, alliance fosters political trust and social community. But there is a countervailing effect: The delegation of security responsibilities by one nation to another is also likely to excite suspicions of abandonment and betrayal. Conversely, the attempt by a nation's political authorities to exact sacrifices from its citizens for the defense of others' citizens may be too severe a test of their legitimacy. It is a delusion of those who "make" policy to think they can commit their own political system to the ultimate protection of other countries and other peoples. The policies and actions of state are not the imagined or promised responses of a handful of elites that purport to represent that state. What, after all, is "committing" about a commitment? A commitment, somewhat like a policy, is a sort of prediction we make about the behavior of our own system. It is a condition that makes it more probable that, in certain contingencies, a country will respond in certain ways. Thus, the quality of commitments depends on complex and objective factors, many of which are quite beyond the control of presidents and other decision-"makers." That is why America's allies must eventually hedge against the promise of American support, either by creating their own nuclear force, as France has done, or by finding other protectors, or by accommodating their adversaries in various degrees (some perhaps quite innocuous). Actions such as these will cause the effective dissolution of the alliance, even if the diplomatic forms are preserved, even if no one notices or admits what has happened.

Whether America will fight for Europe, or whether it will in some way use the territorial depth of Europe as a buffer, is not a subject of polite conversation between Americans and Europeans. But decoupling from Europe is America's "secret" strategy. Not, of course, in the sense that our leaders are keeping it a secret, but rather because strategy (somewhat like "policy") consists of what a nation—a complex political-social system—will do at the time that strategy must be invoked, not what its leaders profess or prefer, or even what they might have "planned" to do.

Europeans already suspect this. Virtually every American strategic move—up, down, or sideways—has evoked the specter of decoupling in one or another of its forms; either the avoidance of a nuclear response altogether or the attempt to confine even a nuclear conflict to the European theater. This is not something that began suddenly when President Reagan said: "I could see where you could have the exchange of tactical weapons against troops in the field without it bringing either one of the major powers to pushing the button."[1] The doubts had been sown long before that, in a series of American moves: The MLF (the multilateral nuclear force, the contradictory American scheme to endow Europe with its own nuclear deterrent but with an American finger on the trigger); the emphasis on flexible response and conventional defense by the Kennedy-McNamara administration; the Schlesinger doctrine of 1974, which contemplated the selective use of the American strategic nuclear force; the interest in "mini-nukes," including such variants as the "neutron bomb"; and even the introduction of intermediate-range nuclear weapons, such as the Pershing II and the ground-launched cruise missiles. Though these may enhance coupling by perfecting the essential link of theater nuclear weapons, they may also allow the restriction of nuclear conflict to Europe.

More recently, President Reagan's Strategic Defense Initiative, a design to protect American society from Soviet missiles, has stirred European concern that the United States could afford a "Fortress

America" mentality and ignore forward defense in Europe. And, finally, America's current attempt to endow NATO with "emerging technology" has had the significance, to some Europeans, of further detaching the United States from its commitment to escalate to nuclear weapons, specifically by promising conventional coverage of some targets that now require nuclear systems.

A near-paradox—surely an illustration of the Europeans' propensity to perverse interpretation—is that even too direct coupling can be viewed rather as a kind of decoupling. One would think that the "massive retaliation" doctrine of the early Eisenhower-Dulles administration, which promised direct strategic nuclear response to a Soviet conventional attack on Europe, without intermediate levels of reaction, would be exempt from suspicion. But even that doctrine caused doubt and apprehension among our Western European allies, because it invited a Soviet counterstrike upon the United States and therefore did not constitute a credible guarantee. There is such a thing as too much nuclear deterrence. On the other hand, there is such a thing as too much conventional defense. As Justin Galen noted:

> Any attempt to improve NATO's conventional forces without correcting its growing problems in nuclear capability . . . could cause deep European distrust of the U.S. and European fear of U.S. 'decoupling' of its strategic forces. . . . The LTDP [Long Term Defense Program] has come to symbolize the question in many European minds of how much conventional defense is safe for Europe. . . . Our allies have begun to ask whether the Americans may be increasing NATO's conventional component in order to be able to fight a more protracted conventional war, in an attempt to make Europe a self-contained area of conflict.[2]

At issue here is not whether these American strategic moves are well planned or well meant, but whether they have the effect of attenuating the American connection with Europe; whether they provide reasons, or even pretexts, for the United States to make its escalation to strategic nuclear weapons less than prompt and automatic; whether they give the United States additional buffers or "firebreaks" (a firebreak is any device, strategy, or doctrine that makes escalation to nuclear weapons less than prompt and automatic). Coupling and firebreaks are inversely related. Coupling, across geography and between levels of warfare, is the essence of alliance protection in a nuclear age, but it contradicts the introduction of firebreaks. Firebreaks are an imperative of our security in an era of nuclear parity, but they impair alliance protection. This is more than a simple antithesis; it has the aspect of a paradox, since the enhancement of any level of military recourse can be regarded alternatively as a link to higher levels of escalation and as a self-contained effort. Improved conventional defense can postpone nuclear escalation and widen the firebreak between conventional war and nuclear war. On the other hand, earlier resort to discrete and controlled tactical nuclear weapons invokes the specter of limiting even a nuclear war to European territory, creating yet another firebreak, this one between theater and total nuclear war.

These matters, though they rest on abstract and contingent calculations, are not in the realm of theory or theology. Future hypothetical events affect present military dispositions, the nerve of contestants in crises, the course of diplomacy within the alliance, and the coherence of the Atlantic strategic community. In both logic and fact, the United States has already, implicitly, decoupled from the defense of Europe, in those contingencies that the alliance was established to meet. Thus, NATO has already ceased to function wholly for both parties, America and Europe, and it has ceased to function in the same essential ways for both. Europe's interest, at the center, is to avoid being caught in a quarrel between the superpowers. America's interest, at the periphery, is to avoid being drawn integrally into a conflict that could otherwise be localized in Europe. To the Americans, Europe is an early warning of Soviet intentions in the world, and a temporary barrier; but to the Europeans, of course, it is all there is.

Henry Kissinger was clear and prescient about these matters when he addressed a private gathering of American and European strategists in Brussels in September 1979. In a remark that has since gained wide currency, he permitted himself some pessimistic reflections on the validity of the American nuclear guarantee:

> Perhaps even today, but surely in the 1980s, the United States will no longer be in a strategic position to reduce a Soviet counterblow against the United States to tolerable levels. . . . If my analysis is correct, we must face the fact that it is absurd to base the strategy of the West on the credibility of the threat of mutual suicide. . . . And therefore, I would say, which I might not say in office, that European allies should not keep asking us to multiply strategic assurances that we cannot possibly mean or if we do mean, we should not want to execute because if we execute, we risk the destruction of civilization.[3]

Kissinger's remarks should not have been surprising. Fourteen years earlier, he had pointed out that the disabilities of NATO are not peculiar; they afflict all alliances of sovereign nations. Kissinger discovered virtually a law of alliance: the contradiction of military effectiveness and political sovereignty:

There is an increasing inconsistency between the technical requirements
of strategy and political imperatives of the nation-states. . . . The dilemma
arises because there is no scheme which can reconcile these objectives
perfectly so long as the Atlantic Alliance remains composed of sovereign
states.[4]

The basic contradiction is only sharpened by the advent of nuclear
weapons; and in this there is a further irony. Nuclear technology
permitted extended deterrence in the first place and thus constituted
the cement of alliance. But once the technology is diffused, beyond
the monopoly of one nation, it prohibits extended deterrence and so
becomes the solvent of alliance.

THE LOGIC OF EXTENDED DETERRENCE

The American guarantee to defend Western Europe can scarcely be
evaluated without examining the logic of extended deterrence. Extended
deterrence (as opposed to central, or primary, deterrence) is the attempt
to discourage attacks or pressures against nations and peoples other
than ourselves by threatening the use of our nuclear weapons. Some
would say that NATO, more than other alliances, not only depends
on, but virtually consists of, the extended deterrence provided by its
principal guarantor, the United States. That is perhaps an exaggeration,
but it suggests a fault-line in NATO: The requisites of extended deterrence and the difficulties in achieving those requisites result, to the
extent that we succeed, in danger and expense to the United States,
and yet, to the extent that we fail, in the implausibility of our protection
of Europe.

What are the requisites of extended deterrence? It can be argued
that to validate extended deterrence—that is, to be seen as standing
ready to implement it as convincingly as we do central deterrence—
requires the practical invulnerability of our own society to Soviet attack.
(I say "practical," since absolute invulnerability is beyond anyone's
reach; what is required is to limit damage to "tolerable" levels of
casualties and destruction.) This is so an American president can
persuade others that he would risk an attack on our homeland in the
act of spreading America's protective mantle over Western Europe and
other parts of the world. If we were to seek societal invulnerability,
we would have to work through both our defensive and our offensive
strategic systems. First, we would have to achieve a strategic defense.
This would require measures such as area antiballistic missiles (ABM)
and laser or particle beam weapons in space, air defense against Soviet
bombers and cruise missiles, and antisubmarine warfare against Soviet

submarines (this is the borderline of defensive and offensive damage-limiting measures), and a vast program of shelters and evacuation. These measures are very expensive. Estimates of their overall cost are a vague and moving target, but it seems plausible, from official and unofficial analyses, that the strategic defensive measures needed to protect society (not merely degrade an initial barrage against our missile silos) might cost from half a trillion to a trillion dollars, over perhaps 15 years, if we were to go about them seriously, not just symbolically. And this is entirely apart from the questions of whether such defensive measures are technically attainable, and sustainable against Soviet countermeasures, and whether they would provide sufficient impermeability against the sheer multiplication of offensive vehicles and warheads.

As a second condition of societal invulnerability, we must be able to hold in reserve, after any of the earlier stages of a protracted nuclear exchange, enough destructive power to threaten countercity strikes, so the enemy would never with relative impunity threaten to attack our cities and exact a political price that might include our surrender. This means that the United States must have redundancy of nuclear weapons, and that they must be survivable.

Finally, a mostly indirect but very significant requisite of societal invulnerability is the acquisition of a nuclear counterforce capability, specifically hard target kill. Counterforce contributes to damage limitation in several related and mutually reinforcing ways, both indirect and direct. High accuracy in our missiles, great destructive power in our warheads, and the capacity of our missiles to carry large numbers of independently targeted reentry vehicles (MIRVs or equivalent numbers of single warhead missiles) would enable us to execute a damage-limiting strike against the Soviets' "time-urgent" nuclear forces, primarily their missiles in silos. Thus—*indirectly* damage-limiting—our counterforce capability would erode the enemy's ability to attack American nuclear forces; in turn, American nuclear forces would survive in larger numbers, the better to deter the enemy's eventual attack on our cities by holding his own cities hostage. And—*directly* damage-limiting—our counterforce capability would erode the enemy's ability to attack our cities in his earliest response, if that were, irrationally, to be his move.

Thus, America's drift to counterforce is not perverse or accidental, as some critics would represent it. Ultimately counterforce, just as strategic defense, proceeds from our adherence to alliance commitments. Yet the requirement for a counterforce capability has two liabilities: It is open-ended, and it is unstable. First, it is a most demanding nuclear strategy. Implying, as it does, hard target kill, it is responsible for the major part of the current ideal deployment of 15,000 to 20,000 reentry vehicles (RVs) in the U.S. intercontinental strategic nuclear force (this is in addition to cruise missiles, short-range attack missiles, and bombs carried by bombers), and thus for the present expansion of our nuclear force levels toward those goals.

Second, counterforce, to have its intended effect, must be preemptive. Indeed, counterforce and first nuclear strike are mutually dependent. A first strike implies counterforce targeting, since the only initial attack that makes sense is a damage-limiting strike, the destruction of as much of the enemy's nuclear force as possible. In return, counterforce targeting implies a first strike, a preemptive attack, because a second strike against the enemy's missiles is useless to the extent that our missiles would hit empty holes.[5]

Why would the United States have opted for this demanding and destabilizing strategy? Several proposed rationales are not entirely convincing or complete. A frequently stated purpose is to "neutralize" the Soviets' hard target kill capability. If this implies just symmetrically matching their nuclear force, it is meaningless. If it means acquiring an effective first strike capability and designing to use it, it is quite another matter, and falls into a rationale that is explored below.

A more interesting rationale is to induce crisis stability (a state of affairs where, even in the midst of a developing confrontation or even a conventional war, neither side has an incentive to initiate the use of nuclear weapons). In this explanation, our counterforce deployment would threaten Soviet fixed land-based missiles and thus force the Soviets to redeploy those missiles to sea or, second-best, to land-mobile basing, thus eventually leading to the reciprocal invulnerability of both sides' nuclear forces and so ensuring crisis stability. But even this more attractive rationale for counterforce is tenuous. For this more stable state of affairs would exist only at the end of a long process that must pass through a phase of acute *in*stability. Since no basing mode for our land-based counterforce missiles would credibly confer invulnerability, our attainment of hard target kill capability would be correctly construed as a first strike posture. The Soviets might initially react by planning to launch their threatened missiles on warning, or even preemptively. On the other hand, even if our nuclear counterforce were to force the Soviets to move to an invulnerable posture, this could actually be counterproductive to the specific national strategy favored by those who also favor counterforce. For, if it were to achieve its intended effect of crisis stability, it would undermine American deterrence of conventional aggression, because such aggression would be sheltered under a more crisis-stable nuclear roof. Since neither the United States nor an aggressor would have sufficient incentive to escalate, an adversary might more readily seek—and the United States would have to accept—the verdict of a conventional war. In any case, if all we wanted from counterforce was to establish crisis stability, there are more direct ways to do this. We could achieve this unilaterally, by removing our fixed land-based missiles (Minuteman) and not replacing them with mobile or multiply-sheltered or super-hardened follow-on systems such as MX, or even the proposed dispersed, single-warhead Midgetman.

In fact, as we have noted above, the compelling motive for counterforce, as well as strategic defense, is damage limitation—that is, limiting the damage to the United States in a nuclear war. And this motive in turn springs from the requirements of extended deterrence. Any strategic policy will try to protect certain values that are at the core of our national identity and sovereignty. These values include our political integrity and autonomy and the safety and domestic property of our people. These are the proper—and largely feasible—objects of American defense or deterrence. It is when we attempt to protect more than these objects with our strategic nuclear force that we court the peculiar problems of *extended* deterrence. Then the calculus of credibility that we make with regard to strict central deterrence does not hold. The assumptions of deterrence apply to peripheral areas and less-than-vital interests with much less strength and validity.

At one time, in the early 1950s, it was thought that nuclear deterrence, once achieved by the United States, could scarcely be denied to any ally, and could be extended to all allies without incremental cost. In other words, nuclear deterrence was thought to possess the dual characteristics of a public good: nonexclusiveness of distribution and jointness of supply. It was both universal and cheap. Those aspects of nuclear deterrence underpinned the economy of massive retaliation. Combined with wall-to-wall security alliances (pejoratively labeled "pactomania"), nuclear deterrence could substitute efficiently, it seemed, for actual defense.

What was neglected were some entailments. (Indeed, it is not the "first-order" effects of alliance that will bring about its rejection, and rarely soon. Rather, it is the "second-order" effects, sometimes only tenuously associated, or not at all associated, with the alliance, yet objectively caused by it—the risks, exhibited in occasional crises and confrontations, and the costs, exacted in the form of taxes or, alternatively, inflation—that may be rejected by a society, and, because the second-order effects are entailed by the assumption of alliance, their rejection will bring the continuance of alliance into doubt.) The extension of deterrence to Europe (and other areas) brought greater exposure to risks, multiplication of occasions for intervention in conflict, implication in the internal affairs of the states that we acquired as proteges, and the periodic pledge of our cities in the support of each threatened or anxious client.

The connection between the United States' ability to protect itself and its ability to protect allies is not generally well understood. For it is not the problem of deterring a direct and initial nuclear attack on the United States that is at stake here. That is not nearly as likely or elusive a case. First of all, the scenario, the circumstantial linkage, for such a direct and initial nuclear attack on the United States is highly unlikely by comparison to, say, an initial conventional invasion of Europe; and our finite second strike capability against value targets (even if only military-related value targets) in the Soviet Union would be a sufficient—or sufficiently credible—deterrent: The Soviets must believe that an American president would retaliate against a direct attack on his own country, not just on allies. In any case, for this direct and essential *deterrent* purpose, societal invulnerability is close to irrelevant; it is designed to protect, not to deter, and, by definition, the Soviets would already have attacked the United States (though they might have tried to limit their attack to a disarming strike against our nuclear forces). Certainly, in that circumstance, for direct and essential deterrence, the component of societal invulnerability that might be provided by our counterforce capability would be virtually useless; it would even be far less useful in limiting damage.

Rather, the case for our attainment of societal invulnerability concerns the validity of our guarantee to defend allies—that is, the efficacy of *extended* deterrence. This is a point that is made most insistently by those who are identified with the resolute pursuit of nuclear warfighting and strategic defense. One formidable sequence comes from the commentary of Colin S. Gray and Keith Payne:

> The credibility of the extended U.S. deterrent depends on the Soviet belief that a U.S. president would risk nuclear escalation on behalf of foreign commitments. . . . The commitment to preserve Western Europe against aggression . . . requires American strategic forces that would enable a president to initiate strategic nuclear use for coercive, though politically defensive, purposes. . . . U.S. defense planners [now] do not consider anticipated damage to the United States to be relevant to the integrity of their offensive war plans. The strategic case for ballistic missile defense and civil defense has not been considered on its merits for a decade. . . . It would not be in the interest of the United States actually to implement an offensive nuclear strategy no matter how frightening in Soviet perspective, if the U.S. homeland were totally naked to Soviet retaliation. . . . No matter how grave the Soviet offense, a U.S. president cannot credibly threaten and should not launch a strategic

nuclear strike if expected U.S. casualties are likely to involve 100 million or more American citizens.[6]

These authors draw the threat clearly from extended deterrence through societal invulnerability all the way to nuclear war-winning, presuming counterforce targeting and preemptive strike.[7]

To list, and demonstrate, the requisites of alliance is not to argue for any of these implementing measures. Quite the contrary, it is to show how our weapons and our strategic doctrines, far from being mindless, are closely dictated by our alliance responsibilities. Conversely, our willingness to protect allies rises and falls generally with our ability to protect our own society from nuclear attack and, more specifically, with the prospective viability of counterforce. To the extent that there is any explicit doubt—technical, economic, political—that we will achieve that invulnerability or that we should pursue counterforce (and I believe the foregoing discussion indicates that there should be such doubt), there is an implicit doubt that our extensive nuclear commitments, especially to Western Europe, can survive.

COST AND RISK

What emerges from this analysis is that the attempt to implement extended deterrence—to defend, say, Western Europe efficiently and thoroughly by substituting the threat of nuclear weapons for the conventional defense of the theater—requires conditions which, if they can be fulfilled at all, are expensive or dangerous or counterproductive. Therefore, extended deterrence does not confer a cheap and painless advantage. It is just one of an array of stark, primal strategic choices.

What are those fundamental strategic choices? In general terms, a country that has undertaken the obligations of alliance faces a series of options:

- It could assume the burdens of high-confidence conventional defense, with the necessity of preparing large and timely reinforcements.
- Or it could accept the risks of substantial reliance on nuclear deterrence, including the option of first use; that is, it could lower the nuclear threshold, or just keep it at an already low level.
- Or it could admit the prospect of conventional defeat in the theater, without escalating or reinforcing.
- There is, of course, another alternative: it could lower the required level of defensive effort. This could be done either by arms control (mostly conventional) that would truly bind the adversary and thus

reduce the threat—if this is attainable—or by disengagement from our commitments to defend other countries. The nation could disengage partially, by devolving some defensive responsibilities to allies or proxies, possibly with a compensatory transfer of arms (this, in its time, was called the Nixon Doctrine); or it could disengage entirely, by sloughing off military alliances.

There are no other ways to go. The alternatives, to a certain extent, can be mixed or substituted; cost and risk can be traded off, within a certain range. But they cannot be transcended; and what they entail cannot be evaded. The "choices" a complex society or political system makes are not always explicitly declared, but they are made nonetheless. For example, to the extent that an administration, even one that disguises the logic of its actions with the most artful diplomatic communication, fails to accept the risks of nuclear deterrence or to assume the burdens of high-confidence conventional defense, or fails to negotiate the conventional burdens reliably away (for example, in Mutual and Balanced Force Reduction talks), it implicitly accepts contingent defeat, or even de facto disengagement from the fate of its allies.

In the case of NATO, America's commitment to Europe presents the United States with a more focused choice between unsupportable costs, associated with the confident defense of Europe with conventional forces, and unassumable risks, attributable to reliance on the earlier use of nuclear weapons. The direction in which this tension is resolved, by any particular American administration, is not rigidly determined; to some extent cost can be transmuted into additional risk, and risk can be transformed into mere cost. (That is what is meant by "raising" or "lowering" the nuclear threshold.) But as long as the United States is committed to Europe, the choice, itself, is inescapable.

The Europeans have a somewhat parallel structure of choice: costly generation of sufficient conventional forces, or acquisition or expansion of their own national nuclear arsenals, with the accompanying more resolute and risky doctrines of employment. But there is an obvious difference: The European allies are situated more or less along the forward line of defense, down the center of Europe and in the Eastern Mediterranean; the United States can "decide" (in that diffuse and objective way in which national decisionmaking systems, particularly plebiscitary democracies and polities of dispersed powers such as the United States, decide these matters) whether it wants to pitch its own security perimeter along that common line.

Those factors of cost and risk are shaped by the divergent options, with different sacrifices and penalties, that arise from the relative situations of the United States and Europe. Thus, European allies alternately try to prolong their run of luck in attracting disproportionate American support (the response of nervous governments), and (the response of anxious peoples) try to avoid implication in the American style of defense, which periodically tilts to the substitution of nuclear strategies and the confinement of even a nuclear battle to the European continent. For its part, the United States continually attempts to mitigate the consequences of its commitment; and these attempts tend to diminish the deterrence of conventional war in Europe and to decouple the United States from Europe.

The risks that stem from our extended deterrence inspire attempts to avoid the contingent nuclear destruction of our homeland. Such an attempt is the case against the first use of nuclear weapons, of which the most notable statement in recent times is the 1982 article by McGeorge Bundy, George F. Kennan, Robert S. McNamara, and Gerard Smith, "Nuclear Weapons and the Atlantic Alliance."[8] The latter article is classic, not only in its exposition but also in the problems it incurs in its premises and argument.

Its principal problem is that it insists on maintaining the integrity of the American commitment to the defense of our Western European allies; and yet it seeks to obviate the risk, to the United States, of destruction in a nuclear war. If one is committed, as are Bundy and his fellow authors, both to defend Europe and to avoid the extension of conflict to our homeland, one must try to reconcile these awkward objectives. Thus, crucial in the Bundy-Kennan-McNamara-Smith proposal is that its apparent renunciation of the first use of nuclear weapons is conditioned on the acquisition of an adequate conventional defense.

But those who opt reflexively for conventional defense cannot mean just any conventional effort. They must mean the *high confidence* defense of Europe with conventional arms. And they cannot just exhort or prescribe that the United States and its allies "must" do more to guarantee the integrity of Western Europe; they have the further burden of *predicting* that this will happen.

In order to determine the feasibility—and hence the predictive probability—of the conventional defense option, we must have a bill of costs. But seldom—nowhere in the Bundy article—is that bill set forth. What would the conventional option in Europe cost the United States? One must look first at what we are already spending.

In terms of forces, I judge (from an analysis of Secretary of Defense Caspar W. Weinberger's 1986 "Posture Statement," presented to Congress on February 4, 1985) that, for FY 1986, the Reagan Administration intended the following regional distribution of a total of 21 active ground divisions: NATO/Europe, 11 2/3 divisions; East Asia, 3 2/3 divisions; other regions and the Strategic Reserve, 5 2/3 divisions.

By applying these fractions to the total cost of our general purpose forces, $241 billion, we can calculate the rough cost of our three regional commitments. By my estimates, Europe accounts for $134 billion, Asia absorbs $42 billion, and the Strategic Reserve, including an expanded requirement for the Persian Gulf and Southwest Asia, takes $65 billion. One hastens to point out that the commander in chief of a given unified or allied command does not see all those costs. The American forces that he commands are just the tip of the iceberg; most of the costs involve support units and Pentagon overhead. The money is spent in the United States, but it is attributable to our commitment to defend each specified region.[9]

Our present share of the conventional defense of Europe—and this is not even designed to be a self-contained conventional defense—is about $134 billion for FY 1986. This is 42 1/2 percent of the $314 billion originally requested for defense by the Reagan administration. Given a reasonable projection of current cost growth, over the next 10 years Europe will cost the United States $2.2 trillion. (It may be of some interest to compare this with the fact that, over the 36 years of its existence, the cost of NATO to the United States has been roughly $1.5 to 2 trillion. Each year, NATO-related costs have been between 40 and 50 percent of our defense budget.) The appropriate question is whether even those resources will be forthcoming, let alone the greater ones required for self-sufficient conventional defense.

Indeed, if the United States were to set for itself, and its allies, the task of providing a confident conventional defense against Soviet arms, principally on the central front of Europe, the costs of this, in terms of American defense spending, would be far higher than most proponents of conventional defense are willing to concede. The exceptional estimate of the entailed costs, in necessarily rough terms, has been given by Leonard Sullivan, Jr.: "Expanding our conventional forces by 20% over the next 10 years to offset the numerically, qualitatively, and geographically expanding threat requires that defense outlays rise . . . to 9 1/2% of the GNP . . . (about 1/2% more in TOA [Total Obligational Authority])."[10] That 10 percent, applied to the probable 1986 GNP of $4.17 trillion, would mean a defense budget authorization of $417 billion, not the $314 billion requested. The defense of NATO in 1986 would cost $179 billion instead of $134 billion.

Comparing the relative burdens of the United States and its allies is not the point, and so even adjusting these burdens would not be the solution. The question has always been whether the United States is getting its own money's worth out of its forward strategy, and would be getting its money's worth even after some putative redistribution of burdens. Inevitably, we are thrown back on the economy of alliance.

There are several ways of formulating this equation, or inequality. It may be that the actual costs of our preparations to support and implement the alliance exceed our gains, including as gains the benefits we derive from the contributions of allies. It may also be that, in the calculus of a possible war, the losses we would sustain through not defending forward are less than those we would incur through defending forward, even if successfully (and the value of both outcomes must be cut by their fractional probability, which is far less than certainty), plus the real costs we would have sustained in preparing to defend in that way. And, in the encompassing calculus of deterrence, the future losses we might sustain by not even deterring attack or coercion against forward countries, reduced by the very low probability that such would occur because we failed to deter, might be less than the cumulative costs of deterrence. If we are assessing bargains, those more comprehensive and more complex calculations are the appropriate ones.

To mitigate the heavy costs of committing a portion of our force structure to the defense of Europe, some have proposed the unilateral withdrawal of part of the American forces in Europe. The salient version of this approach was the Mansfield Amendment or Resolution, offered in Congress for eight years until 1975. This proposal, in its various forms, would have reduced American troops in Europe by as much as two-thirds, redeploying them to the United States but not (in all but one year's version) deleting them from the active force structure. But withdrawal of units saves nothing unless they are also deactivated. Nor would the Mansfield proposal have touched the forces kept in the United States for European contingencies. (Forces the United States keeps in Europe are only about one-third of the forces it maintains for the support of NATO.) Thus, it would have made only a small dent in the amount, $134 billion for 1986, that we spend annually for the defense of Europe. Most significantly, our commitment to European defense would remain in full force. This is not a virtue but a flaw; the Mansfield type of initiative represents withdrawal without decommitment, a precarious stance.

Most versions of troop withdrawal are more trivial, some merely symbolic. An example was the amendment sponsored, in the fall of 1982, by Senator Ted Stevens (R-Alaska), Chairman of the Senate Appropriations Subcommittee on Defense, that would have lowered the ceiling on our deployments in Europe in such a way as to return some 23,000 troops to the United States. Of course, as Morton H. Halperin said, in rebuttal,[11] it is cheaper to keep our troops in Europe. But that is not the end of the debate. Cheaper than what? Certainly it is cheaper than keeping our defensive commitment and just relocating our forces to the United States, providing even more prepositioned equipment in Europe and more airlift and sealift to return our forces there at the first sign of trouble. But it is not cheaper than absolving ourselves of the commitment, disbanding most of the forces we devote to it, and also saving the tactical air and surface naval units that go along with it. If we were to adopt such a nonprotective attitude toward Europe, over a decade of progressive disengagement we could save almost 60 percent of the $2.2 trillion we are now committed to spend on NATO, and, at the end of that decade, we would be spending 80 percent less than we will if we keep on our present course.

Moreover, aside from the cost of substituting self-sufficient conventional defense, and the consequent unlikelihood of achieving this, ironically the attainment of high-confidence conventional defense would defeat the aims of deterrence. For, unfortunately, it is the very fear of inevitable escalation of a local European conventional war to a global nuclear conflagration that constitutes the essential element in the coupling of our strategic nuclear arsenal to the local defense of our allies. Yet coupling is the antithesis of firebreaks. For extended deterrence to work, the escalatory chain, from conventional war to theater nuclear weapons to the use of America's ultimate strategic weapon, must seem to be unbroken; and writers such as Bundy, Kennan, McNamara, and Smith propose to break that chain at the point of the first use of tactical nuclear weapons in Europe.

So the argument of Bundy *et al.*, which started by attempting to obviate the nuclear component of our defense of Europe while preserving the coupling of the United States and Europe, ends by abrogating the coupling that gave rise to the nuclear requirement in the first place. The authors cannot wish away the connection between the first use of nuclear weapons and our defensive guarantee of Europe, without blowing away the defensive guarantee itself.

The Europeans intuit this point quite well.[12] Bundy *et al.*, may *say* that their proposed change "would not and should not imply an abandonment of [our] extraordinary guarantee—only its redefinition." But that remarkable statement remains a hope, not an objective assurance. Indeed, those who propose no first use of nuclear weapons without insuring our successful conventional defense are, despite themselves, implicitly arguing for our disengagement from NATO (or perhaps our relapse, in an extremity, into first use after all; the logic of the article is unstable).

A *consistent* proposal of no first use of nuclear weapons—one that leads to war-avoidance—implies the dissolution of our defensive commitment to NATO. No first use is a requisite, among others, for crisis stability, and in turn for providing elemental safety for the United States (though not necessarily for its present allies) in an age of nuclear parity and nuclear plenty. Of course, deterrence of conventional war in Europe would be diminished; that is, "deterrent stability" would suffer. But it suffers also in the Bundy-Kennan-McNamara-Smith proposal. The difference is that their proposal glosses over the contradiction between crisis stability and deterrent stability. There is an essential tension, not an easy complementarity, between achieving safety for ourselves through crisis stability and achieving safety for the objects of our protection in the world through deterrent stability. The only way we can lessen this tension is by diminishing our obligations to extend defensive protection, in any form. Crisis stability more closely coincides with deterrent stability as we shed external commitments and concentrate on our own defense.

AN ALTERNATIVE PRESCRIPTION
OR AN EVENTUAL PREDICTION?

A thorough and consistent disengagement from Europe would be part of a large-scale reversal of the "paradigm" that has dominated American national strategy for four decades, since the inception of the Cold War: roughly expressed, an interaction of deterrence and alliance—more specifically, extended deterrence and forward defense. This would be replaced by a national strategy of war-avoidance and self-reliance, implemented by our concentration on finite essential deterrence and our disengagement from defensive commitments to other nations.

The United States would shed the responsibilities as well as the burdens of alliance with Europe. Over time, we would devolve defensive tasks upon the European states, but not insist on the orderly and sufficient substitution of capabilities or harbor illusions of maintaining American political weight in European decisionmaking. We would establish a measured and deliberate pace of disengagement and would maintain constructive consultation at all stages. Withdrawal from Europe would probably take a decade of preparation, diplomacy, and logistical rearrangement. But those are modalities, however important they may be. They would not alter the objective of scaling down our forces and setting temporal bounds on our commitment to European defense. We would progressively reduce Europe's strategic dependence on us, and insulate ourselves from the consequences of conflict in Europe.[13]

A question arises about this approach. Is this a prescriptive argument—that the United States should get out of NATO, because of the high costs and unique risks of its defensive commitment? Or is it rather a sort of prediction—that, because of those costs and risks, and the perception by the American political system that they are unsupportable, our commitment to NATO will crumble? Sometimes that question is posed as if reluctance to assign an exclusive definition impairs the argument. But the answers are *both* prescriptive and predictive, and the two reinforce each other even as they are independent of each other.

Much depends on what you think "policy" is. If you believe, as I do, that policy (particularly foreign policy, where the parameters are less alterable and many of the determinants are in the hands of others) is not so much a willful election of goals, or even means, but a prediction of one's own system's contingent behavior over a range of future circumstances, then much of what we call policy-"making" consists of our specific prediction of what those circumstances will be, what alternatives will be available, and how our system will be disposed, and limited, in choosing among those alternatives. That is how prescription and prediction are commingled. American disengagement from Europe is both an alternative prescription and a possible future.

A stance of disengagement proceeds from a prediction of the less satisfactory situation in which foreign policy will have to operate in the future—that is, the more diffused state of the international system—as well as an appreciation of the stringency of domestic constraints—economic, political, and social. Disengagement thus can be viewed as an accommodation to emerging realities in the international and domestic environments of our foreign and military policy.

But most NATO loyalists mistake this kind of critique. One does not have to *urge* the dissolution of NATO, certainly not its instant and formal abrogation. NATO is an alliance that is less dependable year by year, as objective changes in circumstances erode the validity of the essential condition of the alliance: the American guarantee. Conversely, the loyalists should not take as compelling proof of the perpetual durability of the alliance the fact that something called "NATO" has not been formally repudiated. NATO can dissolve without a scrap of paper being torn up, without a journalist reporting it. The failure of almost any of the practical conditions for the integrity of NATO—and that must include the predictive reliability of the American commitment to defend against a wide range of Soviet pressures—will mean the effective demise of the alliance. NATO need not even perish in acrimony. It can expire in skepticism. The strategic content of the alliance can drain away, measured by the confidence allies repose in the ritual American commitment, and by the hedges they erect against the guarantees the alliance still pretends to offer. NATO need not lose its form, at least until long after it has lost its substance. Perhaps the situation can be summed up in a metaphor: NATO, after 36 years, is an old unused medicine on the shelf. The bottle is still there and the label remains the same; but if you ever try it, you find that the contents have long since evaporated or spoiled.

Almost invariably, when one critically or skeptically reviews America's strategic relationship to Europe, people accuse the author of "proposing" to dismantle NATO, and consequently want to know why he would "want" to do such a thing. One might reply that such proposals are no longer so rare as to imply a special animus or an aberrant train of thought. American quasi-isolationists of the right have, in the last several years, made the attentuation of America's protection of Europe, if not exactly respectable, at least not unspeakable or unimaginable. One has only to recall William Safire's pungent formulas:

> The time is coming for an independent European defense. . . . 'Wayward sisters, depart in peace,' Horace Greeley told the seceding states. As Western Europeans turn inward, the U.S. should wish them well and look to its own vital interests.

And this:

> This scenario [of invoking American nuclear protection] is not hooked up to reality. . . . We would pull the biggest Dunkirk history ever saw. . . . The winds of change are growing, in Harold Macmillan's phrase, and will blow our forces homeward. The Europeans will have to choose: to come up with their own conventional defense, or to risk their birthright.

Safire proceeds to outline a Franco-German axis of defense, a "new Gaullism."[14]

Yet I would not want my remarks to be taken as a pure prescription for American withdrawal from the Atlantic alliance. Such a characterization would miss the point and misrepresent the tone of my argument. In short, I am not entirely "proposing." I could do so, but that would be incidental. Instead, a critic such as I is a messenger. Specifically, he is delivering a road map—a decision-tree, if you will (which, in a sense, is what a road map is). He insists only that the recipient see the structure of the problem. To kill the messenger is a response that is traditional, but not therefore less painful or more respectable.

NOTES

1. Interview with out-of-town editors at the White House, October 17, 1981. Bernard Gwertzman, "President Says U.S. Should Not Waver in Backing Saudis," *The New York Times* (October 18, 1981).

2. Justin Galen, "NATO's Theater Nuclear Dilemma: A New Set of Crucial Choices," *Armed Forces Journal International* (January 1979).

3. Quoted in Kenneth A. Myers (ed.), *NATO: The Next Thirty Years* (Boulder, CO: Westview Press, 1980).

4. Henry A. Kissinger, *The Troubled Partnership: A Re-appraisal of the Atlantic Alliance* (New York: McGraw-Hill, 1965).

5. It could be rejoined that a *second* strike counterforce attack would yet be worth conducting, against missiles held in reserve by the Soviets and perhaps against other force targets, and that it could be enhanced by real-time strategic reconnaissance and rapid retargeting. Indeed, a little-remarked feature of President Reagan's October 2, 1981 strategic arms announcement was the intention to achieve such real-time reconnaissance of Soviet silos. Of course, part of the theoretical attraction of deploying a highly accurate, very potent, and multiply MIRVed missile such as MX in a mobile or plural mode, or with ballistic missile defense—or, for that matter, the attraction of many dispersed, mobile, single-warhead missiles such as Midgetman—is that this would promote the substantial survival of such a system and might give the United States the residual weapons, after absorbing a Soviet first strike, to attack Soviet missiles that had not yet been fired. One objection to such a strategy is that our second strike counterforce attack against missiles would encourage the enemy to launch his remaining missiles before they were destroyed. But, beyond that objection, the enterprise of second strike counterforce can be bracketed by two ironic propositions. First—true—the less vulnerable are American forces, the less efficient a Soviet first strike would be, and the more missiles the Soviets must expend in such an attack; but, by the same token, the fewer missiles the Soviets would be able to reserve, and thus the less needed and the less valuable becomes an American counterforce retaliation, though it is more feasible. On the other hand, the more vulnerable are American forces, the more efficient a Soviet first strike, and the fewer missiles the Soviets would need to expend; but the more missiles they would hold in reserve, and therefore—true—the more valuable it might become for the United States to prepare for a second strike counterforce mission, *but* the less viable, since the United States would have correspondingly fewer surviving nuclear forces to execute that mission. (In this framework, the Reagan administration's rejection of mobile or multiple basing for the MX in favor of a fixed deployment—and of a smaller number—reinforces the presumption of an American first strike.) This rather abstract logic does not, of course, completely invalidate the notion of second strike counterforce; there remains some absolute possibility that an American second strike against remaining Soviet missiles would be marginally productive. But the logic does serve to impugn the net value of such a strategy, and thus its plausibility as a motive, or as the dominant motive, for our seeking to attain a counterforce-capable posture and for our concomitant move to counterforce targeting doctrines.

6. Colin S. Gray and Keith Payne, "Victory is Possible," *Foreign Policy* (Summer 1980). See also Colin S. Gray, "Presidential Directive 59: Flawed But Useful," *Parameters* (March 1981).

7. Another serious attempt to integrate the acquisition of counterforce capabilities and the integrity of NATO is made by Edward N. Luttwak, "The Problems of Extending Deterrence," in *The Future of Strategic Deterrence* (London: International Institute for Strategic Studies, Adelphi Paper No. 160, Part I, Autumn 1980, from a conference in September 1979). Luttwak's connection of counterforce and alliance is more direct than that of Gray and Payne, *loc. cit.*, in that it does not proceed as explicitly through the condition of societal invulnerability. Luttwak posits intercontinental counterforce as specifically necessary for U.S. extended deterrence in Europe, to counter Soviet theater nuclear weapons such as SS-20. Both (1) *inter-continental* weapons and (2) counter*force* weapons are needed, as something more than our eroding battlefield nuclear weapons, and even more than our theater nuclear weapons (to which the Soviets could respond, without escalation, with their theater nuclear weapons), and as something less than our implausible countervalue strategic nuclear deterrent. Luttwak's criteria for an effective deterrent are that it must (1) threaten the initiation of wider conflict and (2) be more frightening to a potential aggressor than a potential victim. Those are sensible criteria, though perhaps not conclusive, since it remains possible that some suicidal threats could have sufficient credibility to deter. In any case, Luttwak's argument, in much the same ways as that of Gray and Payne, tends to reinforce the analysis I am offering here: that, if the United States cannot—or, for other reasons, should not—attain or plan to exploit an intercontinental counterforce capability, then the integrity of our defensive guarantee of Western Europe is essentially impaired.

8. McGeorge Bundy *et al.*, "Nuclear Weapons and the Atlantic Alliance," *Foreign Affairs* (Spring 1982).

9. A more ample explanatory section appears in Earl C. Ravenal, *Defining Defense: The 1985 Military Budget* (Washington, DC: Cato Institute, 1984). These figures are in terms of originally requested budgetary authority, not final Congressional authorization or projected or actual outlays.

10. "The FY 84 Defense Debate: Defeat by Default," *Armed Forces Journal International* (May 1983).

11. Morton H. Halperin, "Keeping Our Troops in Europe," *The New York Times Magazine* (October 17, 1982).

12. See the rejoinder to the article of Bundy *et al.*, by Karl Kaiser, George Leber, Alois Mertes, Franz-Josef Schulze, "Nuclear Weapons and the Preservation of Peace: A German Response," *Foreign Affairs* (Summer 1982).

13. What would happen to our present European allies? Western Europe, even without American protection, would not automatically be overrun by Soviet forces, or intimidated into political subservience to the Soviet Union. The countries of Western Europe, even if not formally united in a new military alliance, have the economic, demographic, and military resources, and the advantage of natural and man-made barriers, to defeat or penalize crucially a Soviet attack. See the more extended treatment of this problem in Earl C. Ravenal, *NATO: The Tides of Discontent* (Berkeley, Ca: University of California, Institute of International Studies, 1985).

14. William Safire, "NATO After Grenada," *The New York Times* (November 13, 1983); and William Safire, "Winds of Change," *The New York Times* (April 2, 1984). The former German Chancellor Helmut Schmidt has also sponsored such a "Franco-German security initiative," though not as a total substitute for American forces and the American nuclear guarantee; Schmidt's proposed joint defense, calling for a conventional force of 30 French and German divisions as well as the extension of French nuclear protection over Germany, is designed to raise the nuclear threshold and relieve some American troops. (Speech to the Bundestag, June 28, 1984.)

3

ECONOMIC RELATIONSHIPS AMONG THE ALLIES: SOURCES OF COHESION AND TENSION

James P. O'Leary

INTRODUCTION

The North Atlantic Alliance has, by any fair estimation, attained its fundamental objective: the assurance of peace in Europe. Nevertheless, the Alliance confronts today a combination of serious strains which, in the opinion of many observers, threatens its very existence. Recent disputes over Pershing II missile deployments, followed by controversies concerning the Strategic Defense Initiative and "zero option" proposals, have once again highlighted the essential ambiguity of the Alliance. NATO, in theory and in the view of its principal guarantor, is designed to ensure the conventional defense of the West, *if necessary*, by escalating to nuclear exchanges. Such commitments are enshrined officially in NATO's Long Term Defense Program adopted in 1978 and in national assurances provided biennially in the NATO Force Goals. But this understanding is contradicted by the allies' preference for *rapid* escalatory threats, a reliance on the nuclear option which has served to postpone critical—and costly—conventional buildups and which has produced an unprecedented imbalance in force postures. Given this contradiction, any perceived progress in superpower arms control negotiations raises familiar Western fears of U.S. "detachment" from the nuclear defense of Europe, while any perceived deterioration in superpower relations heightens the fear of devastating war in the Western European theater.

These familiar tensions are today exacerbated by an unprecedented Soviet military buildup and expansionist power projection throughout the globe. Such apparent aggressive designs have arisen precisely at a time of economic sluggishness, high unemployment, and lingering inflationary pressures in many countries. The NATO Alliance is largely a grouping of sovereign welfare states which must grapple simultaneously with new and potentially costly foreign policy challenges precisely at a time when the ability of the welfare state to expand levels of productive output has become highly problematic. Economic tensions have posed serious dilemmas for the members of the NATO Alliance since its inception. But the past decade of stagnation, mounting bilateral trade deficits, wildly gyrating currency valuations and attendant sectoral protectionist pressures have posed an unprecedented challenge to the Western nations (and, of course, Japan). Many observers have voiced fears that short-term economic disarray will inevitably sap the political will of the NATO countries and render the Alliance incapable of adopting long-term politico-military cooperation. Concern that sclerotic economies can no longer sustain large-scale defensive/offensive forces have proven a potent source of support for a variety of "peace" movements and a pervasive climate of pacifism in public opinion.

This problem is exacerbated by the fact that economic problems in the West and the difficulty in competing in hotly competitive areas of world trade have promoted a more favorable inclination in Western Europe towards expanded East-West trade. Such trade provides assured markets with a minimum of competitive pressures. U.S. alarm at expanded economic dependencies between West and East, which erupted most visibly in the pipeline controversy early in the first Reagan Administration, persist albeit in a more muted fashion. Finally, sharp differences between the United States and our allies persist over questions of U.S. policies toward the Third World, U.S. counterterrorism initiatives, U.S. positions on Palestinian rights, insurgencies in Angola, Namibia, Nicaragua, and even Grenada.

In the pages that follow, no attempt is made to deny the seriousness of these issues. Instead, the argument will focus on two economic dimensions of current and future alliance policy. First, the likelihood that current economic strains pose a serious immediate threat to NATO cohesion is assessed. Second, those long-term economic trends which will likely impact seriously upon the Alliance are explored. The purpose is neither to review the past record nor propose a grand strategy for "collective economic security" to complement, and undergird, collective military and political security arrangements. Instead, it is to set forth, albeit in a tentative and inevitably somewhat speculative manner, what appear to be several of the most important long-term forces, operating both at the *microeconomic* and *macroeconomic* levels, which are shaping the future environment of U.S.–Western European–Japanese economic relations. Specifically, this paper (1) reviews the problems posed by protectionism and identifies those trends in trade and investment which represent potentially important *counterprotectionist influences* at the microeconomic/sectoral levels; and (2) reviews recent overall trade and investment trends at the macroeconomic/structural level of the global economy which will affect the longer-term stability and interdependence of the U.S.–Western European relationship. The first section of the discussion is guardedly optimistic about the capabilities of the Alliance membership to resist, or at least contain, mounting pressures for debilitating protectionist "beggar-thy-neighbor" policies. Nevertheless, long-term macrostructural trends in the global economic system, as discussed in the second section, present a potentially more somber scenario.

THE THREAT OF PROTECTIONISM: THE CURRENT SITUATION

Just as the extraordinary appreciation of the U.S. dollar which peaked in March 1985 has been blamed for more than half of the overall U.S. trade deficit (of nearly $150 billion in 1985), so, too, the decline in the dollar since February 1985 has encouraged the belief that currency adjustments alone may go far toward curbing the growth of protectionism among the major Western powers and Japan. It remains the case that the trade tensions which have troubled intra-Allied relationships are rooted in sectoral maladjustments which will not be appreciably altered by currency "corrections": problems of subsidized overproduction in agriculture; inefficient and declining basic manufacturing industries, and hotly competitive pressures in more sophisticated technological sectors will persist. Persisting differential inflation rates among the Western economies may be expected to continue to complicate trade relations as currencies realign. Differences in productivity remain substantial. Annual productivity growth during the last eight years averaged 0.7 percent in the United States versus 3.4 percent in Japan, and 1.8 percent in Western Europe. High rates of unemployment within the major European NATO countries, coupled with their generally more socialist/social democratic political orientation, can be expected to continue to cause trade frictions as countries compete to increase exports and curb imports in an attempt to alleviate unemployment strains. Finally, competitive pressures from Newly Industrializing Countries (NICs, such as South Korea, Taiwan, and Hong Kong), whose currencies are held to the dollar and from heavily indebted Third World nations which are compelled to increase export earnings in order to service mounting debt burdens, can be expected to continue into the medium term future, regardless of currency adjustments. Indeed, to the extent a cheaper dollar will curtail U.S. purchases of imports

from abroad, the locomotive effect of the U.S. trade deficit will diminish, potentially exacerbating global employment and debt-servicing
capabilities.

In short, the deep-rooted structural nature of global trade problems
cannot be denied and no "quick-fix" can be confidently anticipated.
Nevertheless, it is possible to identify a number of significant influences
evident in the contemporary global political economy which might
curb, to some degree, protectionist pressures.

Counterprotectionist Forces Among the Industrialized Nations

The influences which have created sporadic bursts of protectionist
measures and associated rhetoric during the last decade are deep-seated
and aggressive. Nevertheless, important countervailing forces have also
emerged which have thus far blunted the slide toward trade wars and
international financial chaos feared by many otherwise sober observers
of world economic conditions. A brief review of these counterprotectionist trends confirms several of the advantages which the diversified,
pluralistic Allied democracies enjoy in the present economic difficulties.

The "Import Imperative." The economies of the Allied nations are
increasingly constrained to import essential finished goods and intermediate inputs. This "import-or-die" imperative places serious obstacles
before those who would embrace protectionist measures as even a
short-run palliative. Constraints upon the nation's ability to import
freely would prove ruinous for many key economic sectors.

Paradoxically, perhaps the best illustration of the import imperative
is steel. The Reagan Administration, on the eve of the 1984 elections,
announced its import quota "relief" program designed to limit overall
imports, to 20.2 percent of the U.S. market. Given the ominous implications of this quota scheme, it is not surprising to find countervailing forces organizing to limit or to circumvent the new plan.
Importers and foreign suppliers rushed to ship goods in advance of
the new quotas. As importers recently have begun to approach the
limits of their allotted quotas, pressures have mounted on the Administration. In addition, importers of unprocessed flat-rolled sheet
steel (covered by the quotas) have resorted to having the steel fabricated
abroad before importing, thus skirting the quotas and not incidentally
doing serious damage to the U.S. steel fabrication industry. Finally,
and perhaps most undermining to the quota system, many major steel
producers are preparing to lobby for increased quotas for imports from
those countries in which they have subsidiaries or joint-venture partners
and from whom they seek to import finished or semifinished products.

While it is too early to judge the relative powers of the proquota
and antiquota sectors, there is indisputable evidence of growing and

increasingly organized antiprotectionist movements both in the U.S. market and in the economies of our principal Western allies.

Foreign Direct Investment and Joint Venture Projects. Trends in foreign direct investment flows provide a second potent source of counterprotectionist sentiment. The most recent benchmark survey on U.S. Direct Investment Abroad (USDIA) revealed that, as of 1977, there were 3,540 U.S. multinational firms operating 35,789 foreign branches and affiliates. The reasons usually adduced to explain such investment include the desire to "leap over" tariff and nontariff barriers to one's products by locating operations within those markets which offer promising growth prospects; the intent to capitalize on less expensive foreign sources of labor, transportation, or materials, often as part of coproduction strategies; the desire to utilize foreign expertise in managerial and related fields; and the search for preferred access to foreign sources of technology. Pursuit of overall diversification of holdings and productive capacity by means of foreign market penetration and intercorporate collaborative arrangements is growing. Whatever the causes of these investment trends, the facts of increasing foreign direct investment outflows and coproduction/joint venture arrangements in West Europe, the Newly Industrializing Countries, Japan and Canada are clear.

1. West Europe. By 1984, West European countries accounted for 44 percent of all USDIA. The United Kingdom alone accounted for more than 13 percent; other major host countries include Germany (6.5 percent), Switzerland (6.8 percent), the Netherlands (3.5 percent), and France (3.0 percent). Total USDIA in the 10 countries of the European Community (EC) was more than $78.8 billion in 1984, exceeding 34 percent of total USDIA of $233 billion.

In general, future prospects for expanded USDIA in Europe remain clouded by uncertainties. Much of the postwar explosive growth can be attributed to postwar replacement investments; moves to expand production behind EC tariff barriers; efforts to capitalize on internally liberalized and growing markets; restoration of currency convertibility; and free repatriation of earnings. Beginning in the early 1950s, there occurred a general shift of USDIA toward developed Allied countries such that, by 1977, 75 percent of total USDIA was concentrated in the developed countries of Europe, Canada, and Australia. Since 1977, these trends have shifted away from the NATO Allies to favor the developing countries of Asia and Latin America. Controlling for the special case of negative investment in the Netherlands Antilles, USDIA in the developing countries would have grown at twice the rate of increase of USDIA in the developed countries to represent 29 percent of total USDIA.

2. The Newly Industrializing Countries (NICs). It may further be projected that USDIA will flow in the direction of the more developed Newly Industrializing Countries (NICs). Recent analyses suggest that new investments are related more to efforts to market products locally or regionally, as opposed to new investments intended to open up new sources of supply for raw materials. Those investment flows targeted toward selling in local or regional markets tend to be directed at the better-off NICs which enjoy larger per capita incomes and better potential for long-term growth. The principal host countries among the NICs include: Argentina, Brazil, Hong Kong, Mexico, the Philippines, Singapore, South Korea, and Taiwan. During the period 1977–82, the average annual rate of growth of USDIA in these eight countries alone was 13.3 percent in contrast to the rate of growth of USDIA in the developed countries (8.2 percent) and the developing countries as a whole (10.8 percent). During this same period, USDIA globally increased by about $12 billion, a figure which represents 16 percent of the total increase in the U.S. stock of foreign investment. By 1984, 11.5 percent of total USDIA, approximately $26.8 billion, was located in these eight NICs.

It is especially significant that the recent spate of problems associated with international indebtedness has begun to create a climate of greater receptivity on the part of the NICs to increased equity (and portfolio) investment from all sources. Equity investment offers an important source of capital infusion without associated debt service obligations. An increased receptivity to foreign capital investment on the part of host governments could result in a substantial growth in the coming decade of USDIA in these critical NICs of the Asian-Pacific rim and the Western Hemisphere.

From 1966 to 1984, most of the growth of USDIA has been concentrated in Hong Kong (from $126 million to $3.8 billion); Singapore (from $30 million to $2.2 billion); South Korea (from $42 million to $823 million); Taiwan (from $58 million to $828 million); Thailand (from $51 million to $967 million). With the exception of India, there appear to be no significant *economic* impediments to continued growth in such investment in the coming decades. Investment data, therefore, reconfirm the conclusions, based upon trade flow data, that these nations will most likely predominate as the principal economic partners of the United States into the next century.

3. Japan. USDIA in Japan remained at year-end 1984 a modest $8.4 billion, or 3.6 percent of total USDIA. This relatively small proportion may be explained partly by Japanese restrictions on investment which are gradually being reformed or eliminated. Progress in the liberalization of access for investors to the Japanese market

should make Japan one of the most important future areas for USDIA. A concrete example of the potential impact of foreign direct investment flows upon bilateral trade deficits and related protectionist pressures is evident in the current debate over the bilateral U.S.-Japanese trade balance. In spite of the theoretical academic conviction that bilateral deficits in themselves are not *economically* relevant, and that only overall global balances are significant, the magnitude of these bilateral deficits have understandably raised persistent *political* tensions in recent years. Nevertheless, the degree to which such deficits represent one-sided Japanese advantage, vis-a-vis the United States, have been crudely exaggerated. The fact remains that in 1984 approximately $19 billion of "Japanese" sales to the United States represented sales by *U.S.-owner* subsidiaries operating in Japan.[1] Thus, a considerable proportion of the deficit "problem" represents, in fact, the considerable *success* of U.S. foreign direct investors in exploiting their Japanese base to facilitate sales to the U.S. market. In short, in an environment of globalized capital flows, merely to use crude figures of flows of tradable goods as a measure of total economic welfare is to misconstrue gravely the net national advantage accruing from ongoing networks of economic exchanges of investment and trade.

4. Canada. Canada continues to rank first among host countries for USDIA. In 1984, U.S. investment in Canada totaled $50.4 billion, roughly 20 percent of total U.S. investment abroad and a 2.9 percent gain over 1982 USDIA in Canada. Canadian private direct investment in the United States totaled $14 billion in 1984. Because such investment patterns are, after some time lag, historically tied to related trade increases, these investment patterns will likely support increased two-way trade in the future. Prospects for a Free Trade Agreement between the two nations remain feasible despite mounting trade disputes during 1985–86.

Future prospects for USDIA in Canada will depend importantly upon the continued implementation and/or revision of official Canadian policy, as embodied in the Foreign Investment Review Act (FIRA) of 1974 and the National Energy Program. Under provisions of the FIRA, Canadian government approval is required of all foreign acquisitions of Canadian-owned companies. In addition, new foreign direct investment and expansions of existing operations into new industries require approval. Partly in response to the FIRA and the National Energy Program (which favors Canadian-owned petroleum companies over foreign-owned companies), there was net U.S. disinvestment in Canada in 1981 and 1982. Recent events, however, indicate a softening of Canadian attitudes towards regulating direct foreign investments. Given

Canadian capital needs, it may be expected that Canada will continue to host a substantial proportion of USDIA in the coming decades.

5. Overview. The implications of such trends for trade policy choices is clear. In short, any effort to curtail imports from abroad would impact severely upon those firms which have located operations abroad in order to export components or finished goods to the U.S. market. These foreign operations are also major sources of demand for U.S. exports. The proliferation of joint ventures between U.S. and foreign corporations has seriously undermined any clear-cut distinction between "imports" and "domestic" production. Recent initiatives in the automobile industry involving coproduction by General Motors and Toyota, Chrysler and Mitsubishi, and planned cooperation between U.S. and South Korean automobile manufacturers are only the most obvious recent manifestation of an accelerated global trend in investment and production collaboration.

Graphic evidence of the high degree of transnational collaboration due to foreign direct investment flows has recently been provided by Kenichi Ohmae and the international consulting firm of McKinsey and Company. Ohmae has depicted the growing degree of multinational collaboration in the automobile industry, in computer consortia, in air transport, and in biotechnology. In general, Ohmae discovers an emerging trend for distant competitors to merge and share production functions and research and development, leading to a triadic pattern of U.S.–West Europe–Japan interdependence.[2]

Among the conclusions drawn by the McKinsey study, the most thorough empirical review to date of overall trends in foreign investment, is that prudent management can best surmount the "unfortunate political pressures of protectionism" precisely by adopting such strategies of geographic dispersion in order to achieve a true "insider position."[3] To the extent such trends continue, the prospects for growth of the counterprotectionist global perspectives of multinational corporate activities appear promising.

Portfolio Equity Investment Flows. Recent trends in portfolio equity investment flows reinforce the overall picture of heightened interdependencies and growing intercorporate penetration which may serve to blunt incipient protectionist pressures.[4] The globalization of world stock markets has proceeded at a quickened pace in the last decade. U.S. corporations have nearly doubled their listings on the London Stock Exchange from 105 in 1984 to 205 in mid-1985. Of the 2,700 stocks currently listed on the London Exchange, more than 500 are foreign firms. U.S. presence in the Tokyo exchange is currently confined to only 10 companies, but recent studies suggest that this exchange offers the brightest prospects for future U.S. listings.[5] (Market capitalization of stocks on the Tokyo exchange total more than $600 billion, about equal to 40 percent of the New York Stock Exchange and twice the size of the London exchange.) As Japan moves further to ease listing requirements, including costly audits and reporting requirements, sustained growth of this market can be expected.

Overall portfolio equity investment flows confirm the impression of accelerated growth evidenced in the Tokyo and London exchange trends. The rationale for foreign listing of stock offerings would appear to argue for continuation of these trends. Foreign listings can increase the price of a stock by increasing the number of potential shareholders. It is in the interest of current shareholders that the shareholder base be broadened to permit purchases by additional investors. In addition, foreign listings can provide easier access to domestic official and private agencies. This has been a particularly important motivation for listings on the Tokyo exchange where a firm's relationship to the Ministries of Finance and Trade can be significantly advantaged by such a listing. Finally, in this era of merger manias and unfriendly takeover battles, foreign investors provide a measure of support for existing managements resisting takeovers. Foreign investors have thus far proven unwilling to accept payment in the low-rated (albeit high-yielding) "junk bonds" usually used in hostile takeovers to finance tender offers.

The discernible trends, then, argue for a continuation of the interpenetration of foreign equity markets, especially the larger New York, London, and Tokyo exchanges. It can be expected that these crosslistings may reinforce the logic of integration noted in the foreign direct investment sectors discussed above. These mutually reinforcing trends in direct and portfolio investment among firms can create intersecting congeries of mutual interest, fostering *global* perspectives on trade and related matters which may pose potentially powerful barriers to vicious circles of protectionism among and between the major Allies (and Japan).

Trends in International Lending. An additional measure of international economic activity with potentially important consequences for overall trade and economic cooperation is international lending activity. There has been a considerable upsurge in such activities which has seen the former dominance by U.S.-based banks eroded and the role of foreign bankers—particularly Japanese, British, West German, and Canadian firms—expanded. Such financial intermediation has woven an increasingly elaborate network of interdependence between foreign bankers and the fortunes of domestic enterprises. Such ties establish cross-cutting pressures during times of rising trade tensions: The interests of the banking community clearly will not necessarily reinforce the concerns of protection-inclined firms since such actions in the trading sector will have an unmistakably negative impact on a broader range of cross-sectoral financial relationships. To the extent that financial ties embrace both those advantaged by protectionist measures in the short-run but potentially disadvantaged in the long-run (due to retaliation and other consequences of protectionism detailed above), the intrusion of longer-term equity-holding foreign investors *may* militate against such trade distortions. Furthermore, to the extent that protection *invariably* disadvantages a broad range of both import-dependent and export-oriented operations (most obviously those likely to be the target of retaliations), the voices of the financial interests may also be expected to help arrest the momentum of protectionism. Finally, foreign bankers' presence in overseas markets has encouraged the sort of *direct investment* penetration discussed above by facilitating the expansion of home firms abroad.

To the extent these observations hold true, the trends in international banking appear encouraging. Due in part to the fact that foreign bankers enjoy greater leverage (that is, more permitted loans in relation to the banks' capital), foreign banks have been able to charge lower rates of interest than U.S. banks. This competitive advantage—a capital-to-assets ratio of 3.3 percent for foreign banks vs 6 percent for U.S. banks (which may soon be increased to nearly 9 percent by U.S. regulators wary of the Latin American debt crisis)—has yielded a remarkable growth in foreign penetration in the U.S. market and in foreign markets traditionally dominated by U.S. banks. In 1983, foreign bank lending to U.S. companies rose to $84.5 billion (18.3 percent of total U.S. business loans) from $12.8 billion (or 7.6 percent) in 1973.[6] Meanwhile, U.S. bank loans abroad remained slightly down in 1984 from their level in 1983.

The net scenario, then, is one of increasing interdependence between the fortunes of domestic firms and foreign financial interests. Although the picture is not all so optimistic (for example, hotter competition in the banking community has led to questionable loan practices and risky reliance on fees generated by promises to bail out troubled companies), nevertheless, the prospect of increasing interdependence between domestic commercial and foreign financial interests does portend an overall improvement in the prospects for nonconflictual international economic relations and market liberalization within the Atlantic Community.[7]

A Note on Heightened Sensitivity to the Inflationary Consequences of Protectionism. While it is virtually impossible to "measure" the importance of fears of inflationary consequences resulting from protectionism, it is, nonetheless, clear that such concerns represent among the most potent forces countering incipient global protectionist pressures. An especially potent source of counterprotectionist resistance rooted in concerns about inflation derives from those segments of the business community most vulnerable to the price increases attendant upon protectionist policies. For example, the recent decision of the Reagan Administration to impose more restrictive steel quotas has produced substantial opposition from steel importers—including distributors, fabricators, and those industries which have depended upon less expensive foreign steel supplies in order to remain price-competitive. Similarly, as noted above, many industries are simultaneously involved in *both* exporting and importing activities (e.g., major automobile producers which import some models fabricated by foreign subsidiaries and/or joint venture partners). The inflationary consequences of protection are keenly felt even by industries which might otherwise be presumed to enjoy some short-run benefits from such protection.

MACROECONOMIC/STRUCTURAL TRENDS IN THE GLOBAL POLITICAL ECONOMY

Discernible trends in the global world economy suggest a possible shift in the principal axes of world trade and investment from a predominantly "Atlantic" relationship, dominated by U.S.–West European exchanges, toward an Asian-Pacific axis dominated by U.S. trade and investment linkages with the newly industrializing economies of Asia.

West Europe

The prospects for expanded long-term trade and investment linkages between the United States and the principal Allied powers appear problematic: Trade with the European Community (EC) has been sluggish in the early 1980s. While U.S. agricultural exports have fallen dramatically (especially oilseeds, animal feedstuffs, and corn), U.S. imports from the EC soared by 31 percent in 1984. U.S. imports surged across-the-board for all EC countries, particularly from Ireland (50 percent), Italy (46 percent), the Netherlands (37 percent), and Germany and France (35 percent each). Especially sensitive sectors of growing U.S. imports included steel pipes and tubes (231 percent), aircraft (59 percent), specialized industrial machinery (53 percent), petroleum products (46 percent), measuring and controlling instruments (45 percent), and passenger automobiles and motor vehicle parts (33 percent). In part, due to a slow (6 percent) growth in U.S. exports in 1984, the U.S. trade deficit rose from $2 billion in 1983 to $14 billion in 1984.

Obviously, among the most critical factors shaping the longer-term climate for U.S.-EC trade will be the ability of the principal governments to resist protectionist pressures from those sectors worst affected by import surges. For the same reasons detailed above, there is scope for cautious optimism in this regard. Similarly, there has been a strong record of U.S. export performance recently in sales of ADP equipment, office machines, and electronic components (as well as synthetic resins, cotton, rubber, plastics, and nonmonetary gold). These trends indicate that the structure of U.S.-EC trade may be shifting toward reduced agricultural sales to Europe in favor of increased shipments of manufactures, more sophisticated technologies, and services. The ability of the major contracting parties of the GATT to extend GATT rulemaking to agriculture, services, and trade-related investment areas—as called for in the U.S. 1984 Omnibus Trade Act—would provide a major impetus to U.S.-EC trade relations. Such negotiations could also remove—or at least improve—the two most dangerous potential sources of friction (agriculture and services).

Nevertheless, the West European growth scenario is difficult to project. The prospects for a vigorous expansion of high technology venture capital firms is grim given the lack of adequate capital market infrastructure; the deadening effects of official regulations governing new enterprises; heavy subsidization of declining sectors; poor market information networks; and employment protection laws and pension schemes which impede factor mobility. Agriculture is in disarray and the imminent incorporation of Spain and Portugal promises to worsen the already virtually uncontrollable growth of farm surpluses. These surpluses not only drain the EC budget (85 percent of the total budget is currently committed to Common Agricultural Policy subsidies and surplus management programs). They also portend increasing closure of the EC market to any increased exports of U.S. farm products, especially should negotiations for a new GATT arrangement fail. The probability that U.S. farm subsidies will be drawn down as part of an overall budget-cutting scenario opens up the further likelihood of tension as U.S. farm prices fall to market-clearing levels and farmers seek to sell increasing quantities abroad. Perhaps more than in any other trade sector, the possibility of a spiraling vicious circle of protectionism and trade wars threaten agricultural trade in the coming years.

Canada

Canada continues to be the largest trading partner of the United States. The most likely forecast is that this two-way trade dependence will continue. In 1984, Canada accounted for 22 percent of U.S. exports and 20 percent of our imports. Total two-way trade was $113.2 billion of which U.S. exports totaled $35.3 billion and U.S. imports totaled $66.9 billion. In turn, Canada's dependence on the U.S. market has increased; whereas in 1980 sales to the United States represented 63 percent of total Canadian exports, by 1984 sales to the United States represented more than 76 percent of total Canadian exports. Canada enjoyed a $15 billion trade surplus in 1984, attributable largely to automobile shipments ($40 billion in 1984) under existing free trade arrangements and to defense production-sharing agreements. By 1987, when final cuts of the Tokyo Round take effect, fully 80 percent of Canadian exports to the United States and nearly 70 percent of U.S. exports to Canada will be duty-free. Overall, two-way trade has tripled in recent years to more than $110 billion in 1985. U.S. imports from Canada surged 27 percent in 1985, reflecting increased purchases of motor vehicles and parts, internal combustion engines, aircraft, gold, aluminum, and crude petroleum imports.

There are two additional important considerations which argue for a continued high level of trade interdependence between Canada and the United States. First, Canada looms large as a key provider of vital energy supplies. In 1984, the value of U.S. energy trade with Canada was $10 billion. Canada is the principal U.S. foreign source of natural gas and electricity. It is plausible that the overall global decline in commodities and petroleum products will make the dependable U.S. market an attractive asset in Canadian economic planning. Huge oil reserves exist in the Western provinces, which have expressed interest in further lowering existing barriers to trade. Second, the incumbent Canadian government (under P. M. Mulroney) is committed to closer trade integration with the United States. Negotiations for expanded free trade agreements are continuing (especially for liquor, cosmetics, and furniture).

Asian-Pacific Region

In striking contrast with the performance of intra-Allied trade, recent economic performance by the Asian-Pacific countries is impressive. Since 1975, the average compounded growth rate of the five so-called "miracle" countries (South Korea, Hong Kong, Singapore, Taiwan, and Japan) was 8.2 percent, roughly three times the comparable growth rate of the European Community. Similar gains were evident in Indonesia and Malaysia. Since 1978, U.S. two-way trade with the 12 principal friendly powers in the region has grown by 75 percent. In 1983 alone, this trade reached $136 billion, exceeding the $116 billion total for trade between Europe and the United States. While U.S. global trade in 1983 grew by only 0.5 percent, with the Asian-Pacific regions our trade grew by 8 percent. During this period, the Asian-Pacific region also replaced West Europe as the principal foreign market for U.S. agricultural exports. The region now accounts for one-third of total foreign sales by U.S. agricultural producers. In 1984, U.S. exports to the Asian-Pacific region totaled $54.6 billion, while U.S. imports from the region were valued at $114 billion yielding a deficit of roughly $60 billion (versus a deficit of $34 billion in 1983). By 1985 the region accounted for more than 50 percent of the U.S. global deficit and approximately 31 percent of total U.S. trade.

The current investment picture is equally impressive. U.S. investments in the Pacific have an estimated value of $30 billion. U.S. foreign direct investment in the region grew by 65 percent during the 1979–84 period, versus a global increase totaling only 39 percent. Joint ventures are an area of particularly intense activity. Obviously taking advantage of the highly skilled, productive, and relatively inexpensive labor in the region, U.S. businessmen have invested in $16 billion worth of joint ventures in 1984, projected to rise to $28 billion by 1989. The ASEAN countries alone represent the fifth largest U.S. trading partner (behind the European Community, Canada, Japan, and Mexico). U.S. trade with ASEAN grew by 11.5 percent in 1984 over the 1983 total. ASEAN bought $10 billion of U.S. exports in 1984, more than 4 percent of total U.S. export sales.

At the same time that the Asian-Pacific region witnessed unprecedented levels of trade and investment ties with the United States, the region has also enjoyed thriving trade relations among the countries within the region itself. Intraregional trade accounts for well over half the total of exports and imports of the 14 principal trading countries. Perhaps most impressive, fully 70 percent of all developing country exports come from the newly industrializing countries of the Asian-Pacific region.

There are many reasons to expect that the current economic surge throughout the region will persist into the next century. In virtually every respect, fundamental economic conditions are sound. This appears true, particularly when the situation in the Asian-Pacific area is contrasted with that of the other developing countries and with Europe (see below). Of course, the projected sustained economic momentum of the region need not necessarily entail a continued dependence upon the United States as a major trading and investment partner: that will depend importantly on the ability of U.S. business to compete effectively in these hotly competitive markets. Nevertheless, despite such imponderables, it is prudent to expect that this region will hold out the most promise of potential long-term economic ties with the United States for the following reasons:

- The region possesses a huge, skilled, disciplined, and rapidly expanding labor force. This force may be expected to expand by nearly 55 percent by the year 2000 (compared with projected expansion in the United States of only 10 percent).
- This match between an already highly developed technological base and an educated and expanding work force does not appear to be jeopardized by any serious identifiable bottlenecks, especially given current and projected trends in the world energy supply and pricing markets.
- Governments in the region seem generally committed to continuing the prudent domestic fiscal and monetary macroeconomic policies which have thus far encouraged the "economic miracle" of the eighties. Fledgling efforts at official regional cooperation have so far yielded a modest program of cooperative manpower training (only China has abstained from participation).

CONCLUSIONS

As noted at the outset, this essay has attempted merely to map out several dimensions of intra-Allied economic contact which, in the author's opinion, represent potentially critical trends in these relations. Two hypotheses have been proposed for future empirical studies: (1) that counterprotectionist elements are gaining in influence within the major members of the advanced industrial states, and (2) that broader shifts in the nature of U.S.–Western European–Asian/Pacific economic interdependence pose a significant long-term challenge to traditional Atlantic relationships. While overt trade wars may indeed be avoidable given the former development, the latter trend remains a source of concern in the longer run.

NOTES

An earlier version of this chapter appeared in *Power, Principle and Interests,* edited by J. Salmon, J. P. O'Leary and R. Shultz (Lexington, MA: Ginn Press, 1985). Copyright 1985 by James P. O'Leary.

1. The value of the total output of U.S. firms in Japan equaled $44 billion in the same period.

2. Ohmae Kenichi, *Triad Power* (New York: The Free Press, 1985), pp. 134–136, 139, 141–144. Data on the silicon wafer consortia may be found in *Japan Economic Journal* (February 19, 1984).

3. Ohmae, *Triad Power*, p. 209.

4. Direct investment refers to investment made to acquire a lasting interest and an effective voice in the management of an enterprise, while portfolio equity investment usually involves no significant influence over an enterprise's operations.

5. "More U.S. Companies Seek to be Listed Overseas," *Wall Street Journal* (June 10, 1985), p. 6.

6. Source: Federal Reserve Board, *Annual Report* (1984).

7. For example, the greatest allies of the United States supporting the liberalization of Japanese capital markets are precisely the large Japanese banks, insurance companies, and related financial enterprises which perceive enormous potential benefits to result from such an opening up of the Japanese capital market.

4

NO ENTANGLING ALLIANCES? THE CONGRESS AND NATO

Karen A. McPherson

INTRODUCTION

The experiences of the two world wars have generated within the United States a sense of common identity, or at least shared fate, with Western Europe. The American perception of the immutability of the NATO alliance—a perception that reflects in part America's ahistorical approach to international relations—is a root cause of the continuing political problems reflected in the alliance. The fact that the alliance is composed of Western democracies aligned against a common adversary has led many Americans to the erroneous conclusion that the security interests of the member nations of the alliance are identical, and that actions taken to meet the security needs of the United States also address the security needs of the European member nations.

If national security policy were based solely on the functional imperatives generated by events and circumstances in the international arena, that conclusion would be close to reality. In actuality, however, national security policy is significantly influenced by the domestic priorities of the member nations, and these domestic priorities are a function of each nation's history, geographical circumstances, political culture, and economic needs. These domestic influences affect the way the functional imperatives are interpreted. Given the differences that exist within the alliance in these areas, it should not be surprising that the member nations of the alliance want and expect different things from the alliance. The fact that divergent opinions within the alliance continue to cause political turmoil is a reflection less of any inherent weakness in the alliance than of a basic misunderstanding of the factors that drive alliance policy.

FUNCTIONAL IMPERATIVES VS. DOMESTIC CONSTRAINTS IN THE FORMATION OF NATIONAL SECURITY POLICY

The seminal discussion of the process of striking a balance between the demands from the international environment and the constraints from the society is contained in Samuel P. Huntington's *The Soldier and the State*.[1] The demands from the international environment, or functional imperatives, include such things as the capabilities, intentions, and limitations of real or potential adversaries. Balanced against the functional imperatives, in most cases, are the societal constraints that force needs other than defense to be met. Societal constraints, understood broadly, comprise a nation's political culture, which is an outgrowth of its history, geography, resource needs, ideology, and political system. These needs might include, among others, such things as providing funds for social programs and reducing the Federal deficit.

In 1957, when he wrote *The Soldier and the State*, Huntington speculated that functional imperatives would come to dominate societal constraints in the formation of defense policy. Since that time, however, it has become increasingly obvious that societal constraints have a disproportionate impact on defense policy in both the United States and other alliance member nations. One need only look at the establishment of the All-Volunteer Force, the greatly expanded role of women in the services, and the continuing emphasis on personal and civil rights in the military to recognize that societal pressures in the United States are forcing the services to exhibit the same values of the society they are sworn to defend, rather than focus strictly on requirements dictated by the international environment.

The Impact of Functional Imperatives

To say that functional imperatives play a subordinate role in the formation of defense policy is not to say that their role is inconsequential. Alliance members on both sides of the Atlantic are faced with a threat from an expansionist Soviet Union; Soviet actions in Eastern Europe and Afghanistan continue to reaffirm the fundamental military basis of the alliance, an ability to react to Soviet threats. However, the way each member nation reacts to the Soviet threat is conditioned by domestic constraints. The differences in perceptions that so complicate alliance policymaking result from differing domestic filters being arrayed against the international environment.

The Impact of Domestic Constraints

The domestic constraints that influence the national security policy of the member nations of the Atlantic alliance include each nation's geography and history. These factors are particularly critical to an understanding of the differing perceptions among member nations of the alliance.

The geographic separation of the United States from Europe encourages the United States to feel that it has a chance to avoid the next war. From this perspective, strategic reality demands a strategy that does not call for immediate escalation to nuclear war, but allows for some intermediate responses to threats. The geographic contiguity of the European members of the alliance with the Soviet Union, conversely, suggests that any conflict short of an intercontinental exchange of ballistic missiles would be fought out on their territory, with a disproportionately negative impact on people and infrastructure in the area. Thus, for the Europeans, strategic reality demands a strategy that immediately couples any hostilities on the European continent with the U.S. nuclear umbrella.

The doctrine of flexible response was crafted to address these differing perspectives. To the Americans, flexible response allows the nuclear threshold to be raised and admits the possibility of some kind of war on the continent short of an exchange of ballistic missiles. Because they could escape the direct effects of a conventional war fought in Europe, the Americans tend to talk more about the military effectiveness of the nuclear umbrella than its deterrent value. To the Europeans, flexible response commits the strength of the American nuclear arsenal to any conflict in Europe and thus enhances deterrence, which they feel to be the proper role for nuclear weapons. Talk of the military effectiveness of nuclear weapons and the role they might play in defense, rather than in deterrence, makes the Europeans very uneasy.

The historical circumstances that contribute to differing perceptions among members of the Atlantic alliance are an outgrowth of geography, but they are more than geographical in scope. The history of Europe has been one of ebbs and flows of empire, of recurring attempts to achieve hegemony over the continent. Rather than believing, as the United States appears to believe, that the current balance of power in Europe is a permanent fact of political life, the European members of the alliance focus instead on surviving a possibly temporary state of affairs without overreacting and risking total and irreversible alienation of east from west.[2] Whereas to the United States the very thought of bowing to another state is odious, to Europeans this historically has been viewed as a viable alternative.[3]

In addition, history reinforces the perception dictated by geography that the United States has a choice as to whether to be involved in world affairs, whereas Europe has never had that choice. Both the world wars were fought out in Europe; American participation, critical to the successful conclusion of both wars, was not undertaken in response to a direct immediate threat to the safety of its citizenry or the continued existence of its polity.

THE UNEQUAL NATURE OF THE ALLIANCE AND DIFFERENCES IN PERCEPTIONS

If all members of the NATO alliance had an equal impact on the decisions made in the name of the alliance, the fact that these decisions are made on the basis of domestic priorities rather than of objectively determined threats would require an equitable political resolution of outstanding differences of opinion. However, one of the fundamental characteristics of the NATO alliance is that it is not an alliance of equals. The United States is clearly the preponderant power in the alliance; but because of the democratic nature of the members of the NATO alliance, the United States must consult and coordinate the activities it undertakes in the name of the alliance.

The inequalities in the alliance take several forms. It is, first, an alliance of one superpower and many smaller states. It is, second, an alliance in which there are distinctions among the smaller states; Great Britain and West Germany are clearly the "Big Two" of the European members of the alliance. It is, third, an alliance in which the primary means for carrying out alliance military policy, the use or threat to use nuclear weapons, are under the control of the United States. The British nuclear force and the French "force de frappe" notwithstanding, it is the U.S. nuclear capability that provides the muscle behind deterrence. The formal NATO policies relating to the use of nuclear weapons, embodied in the deliberations and statements of the Nuclear Planning Group (NPG), do not mean that the United States has foresworn its independent decisionmaking power over the use of these weapons. The United States does not contemplate a system whereby fundamental control over nuclear weapons is shared; their use could be constrained when the United States might wish to use them, or their use could be compelled against U.S. wishes. Either eventuality is unacceptable, given the nature of nuclear weapons and, perhaps more importantly, the symbology of their use or nonuse. The NATO chains of command are paralleled by national chains of command; for the nuclear-armed members of NATO, decisions relative to the employment of nuclear weapons are likely to come through the national chain of command rather than through the elaborate and cumbersome NATO nuclear release procedures.

Because alliance policies are driven more by the domestic needs of the member nations than by functional imperatives dictated by the external environment, and because the unequal nature of the alliance places the United States in a predominant role, it follows that domestic pressures affecting the United States have a disproportionate impact on alliance policies. The interplay of the various domestic pressures affecting the United States is conducted in the political arena. An understanding of how that arena operates will provide some insight into the political problems that continue to affect the alliance.

THE ROLE OF CONGRESS

The constitutional system under which the United States operates allows several institutional actors to play a role in the formulation and execution of defense policy and budgets. The President, the Executive Office of the President, the Office of Management and Budget, the Department of Defense, the Department of State, and the Congress are the institutional actors whose roles are most important. Because the Congress is the most overtly political of these actors—its 535 members are subjected to direct scrutiny by smaller and more homogeneous constituencies than the broad national constituency of the President, and are thus more likely to act on the basis of parochial political realities—the role of Congress will be the subject of analysis for the remainder of this paper.

The U.S. Congress has both a constitutional right and an obligation to play a role in the formulation of national security policy. The Congress is given the responsibility for authorizing the expenditure of all monies from the U.S. Treasury, including those used to support the military. The power of the purse is not an inconsequential one; policy is carried out through programs and with weapons and supporting equipment that must be funded. In addition, the Senate is responsible for the approval of the appointment of ambassadors and the approval of treaties. The Congress, as a whole, also has the power to declare war.

Reasons for Changes in the Role of Congress

It is from Congress' budgetary role that its present intensive focus on both the substance and process of national security decisions has arisen. In spite of warnings such as that of Senator Richard Russell— "God help the American people if Congress starts legislating military strategy"[4]—since the beginning of the 1970s we have seen a resurgence of Congressional activism.

There are three primary reasons for this change: *First*, the Vietnam War taught many Americans the hazards of unchecked executive power. America's longest war was undeclared and was fought, at least initially, with little functional oversight from Congress. With the passage of the Tonkin Gulf Resolution in 1964, the Congress essentially abrogated its responsibility to oversee policy. It was only as the war was ending, and America was leaving without having accomplished its objectives, that the Congress and the American people began to realize that their government had systematically misled them about the purposes and progress of the war in Vietnam. Public confidence in the institutions of government plummeted; large numbers of Americans came to fear, rather than trust, their government.

Second, the events of Watergate gave further credence to charges of government perfidy. On top of the revelations of the excesses involved in the conduct of the Vietnam War came revelations of outright criminal activity based in the White House. More tempered analysis over the last decade has suggested that President Nixon was following some precedent in his abuse of executive power; Franklin Delano Roosevelt and John F. Kennedy were not above bending the rules to their own benefit. It was the juxtaposition of Vietnam and Watergate that led to the extreme reaction against executive power that was exhibited in the 1970s. Congress felt an obligation to reassert itself as a powerful actor in the policy process.

Third, at the same time, a generational change was occurring in the Congress. During the 1940s, 1950s, and 1960s, an entrenched group of Congressmen and Senators had come to hold positions of great power in the legislature—for example, Rep. L. Mendel Rivers (D-South Carolina) on the House Armed Services Committee, and Sen. John Stennis (D-Mississippi) on the Senate Armed Services Committee— who were strong supporters of the military in Congress. Historical circumstances in the South had led to a situation in which members of both houses from that region were coming to hold positions of great power. The South was virtually a one-party region; the Democrats held the South tightly, and were able essentially to control who held national office. Incumbent Democrats from the South thus tended to be reelected year after year; because committee chairmanships and other positions of power in the Congress were determined by seniority, incumbents of safe seats were able to reach positions of power. These Southern Democrats came to hold many leadership positions; as they were largely conservative and promilitary, the Defense Department was for a long time able to write its own ticket.

However, the passage of time and demographic changes altered this situation. As the older generation of Southern leaders retired, they were replaced by a new breed of Southern politician created by demographic changes that were taking place in the United States in the 1960s and 1970s. The sunbelt states—the South and the Southwest—became recipients of large numbers of Americans who, for economic as well as quality-of-life reasons, were leaving northern cities in droves. As these newcomers arrived in the South, they changed the nature of the population base; the conservative Southern Democrats no longer could control all civic offices. As new officials took the place of those old-line conservative Southern Democrats, they changed the House and Senate in two ways: (1) as newcomers, they were not in positions of power; (2) even as they reached positions of power, they were different from their predecessors: less promilitary, more probing, less willing to give defense a free ride in the budget process. Senator Sam Nunn exemplifies this breed; he is a Southern Democrat, but is nonetheless a leading spokesman for radical defense reform.

General Effects of Congressional Resurgence

As Congress began to reflect these fundamental changes, it was clear that the time was ripe for Congressional reform. In 1974, several procedural changes were made that would make the Congress more able to function as an equal partner with the Executive branch. The seniority system was drastically altered; a "Subcommittee Bill of Rights" was passed to eliminate the overweening power of Committee Chairman. The pendulum has swung before between the Executive and Legislative branches of government; however, this swing brought about the institutionalization of some changes that are expected to make it difficult in the future for the Executive branch to take back lost power.

Renewed Congressional activism made itself felt in the area of defense policy and budgets. The Vietnam War had the effect of creating a surge of interest in the proper role of the military in a democratic society. Congress began to turn its attention to defense matters in response to this new general interest in things military. In addition, throughout the 1970s and 1980s, representatives were elected to Congress whose formative military experiences were not the relatively simple black and white world of World War II, but rather the subtleties, shades of gray, and nuances that characterized the Vietnam era. These representatives are, in general, more probing and more skeptical than their predecessors.

Greater Congressional attention to issues of national defense has changed the character of the defense debate. Because of the nature of its constitutional mandate, the focus of Congressional attention has to be primarily on budgets rather than on issues of overall strategy. For the most part, there is no mechanism by which Congress can make effective pronouncements on issues removed from budgetary concerns. This has always been generally true. Twenty-five years ago, General Maxwell D. Taylor noted: "The determination of U.S. strategy has become a more or less incidental byproduct of the administrative process of the defense budget."[5] Increased Congressional attention to defense has magnified the effects of its budgetary focus. As Congress comes to play a larger role in this area, the debate comes to focus more and more on resource allocation rather than on fundamental issues of policy and strategy. The following statements, made with regard to American support for NATO, illustrate the budgetary nature of Congressional attention to defense policy:

> Our European partners today muster an aggregate GNP over twice that of the Soviet Union. They can and should do more. We must make it plainer than ever before that improvements in American forces in Europe are of little value without significant improvements in Allied forces. (Senator Sam Nunn, 1979)[6]

> For the past 5 years, the committee has placed great emphasis on defense programs oriented to NATO. The United States has paid a price for improvements in NATO war-fighting capability. In the years 1974–1980, in real terms, American expenditures for its NATO forces (including reinforcements) have increased by 3.3 percent per year; and decreased by 1.5 percent per year for all other forces. (Senate Armed Services Committee, 1979)[7]

Examples of what the Congress has done with its newfound muscle provide evidence of the changing nature of the defense debate and illustrate the budgetary "hook" that Congress must find to have an impact on policy:

1. The Cooper-Church Amendment (1970) refused to provide funds for U.S. troops in Cambodia and Laos.
2. The War Powers Act (1973) placed limitations on the President's authority to employ troops abroad in response to crises.
3. The Jackson-Vanik Amendment to the Trade Reform Act (1974) linked trade with Soviet emigration policy.
4. The Clark Amendment (1976) suspended the expenditure of aid funds to Angola.

These actions provide only a few examples of the results of what began with what might be called the "Congressional Spring" of the early 1970s. The impact of this resurgence in Congressional activism has been mixed. Congress has neither the staff, time, nor expertise to examine issues of national defense with the kind of attention to detail that would be required for them to provide a real counterbalance to the flotilla of experts the Department of Defense can access. The primary result of this renewed Congressional attention to defense has been, rather, many more days of hearings on the defense budget, more reporting requirements, more statements and elaborations for the record, and overall, more attention devoted to selling the defense program on Capitol Hill than to enacting it in the Pentagon.

Effects of Congressional Resurgence on NATO

With specific regard to NATO, Congressional activism has been obvious as well. Examination of three issues provides insight into the role Congress has played and continues to play in the conduct of the NATO alliance. They are (1) U.S. troops in Europe; (2) Intermediate-Range Nuclear Forces; and (3) the Strategic Defense Initiative.

U.S. Troops in Europe. When the NATO alliance was formed in 1949, no one perceived that U.S. participation in the alliance would call for the stationing of American troops on a permanent basis on the European continent. President Truman's 1951 decision to station 4 additional divisions in Germany, augmenting the 2 divisions already there on occupation duty and bringing the total number of U.S. troops in Europe to 300,000, created the first controversy over the proper role and numbers of troops stationed in Germany in support of the NATO alliance. Truman's actions provoked great debate in the Senate; Senator Robert Taft fired the opening salvo as he asserted:

(The president) has no power to agree to send American troops to fight in Europe between members of the Atlantic Pact and Soviet Russia. Without authority, he involved us in the Korean War. Without authority, he apparently is now attempting to adopt a similar policy in Europe.[8]

Three days later, Senator Kenneth Wherry introduced a sense of the Senate resolution to prohibit the stationing of American ground forces in Europe in support of NATO until Congress had formulated a policy with respect to such troop deployments.[9] This led to a series of hearings by the Foreign Relations and Armed Services Committees on the issue. Following the hearings, a resolution was passed that suggested the appointment of General Eisenhower as NATO commander and a "fair share" contribution of U.S. forces in NATO; asked the President to consult with the Congress before sending the troops abroad; and asked the Joint Chiefs of Staff to certify that other NATO countries were doing their share before U.S. troops were sent.[10] The Senate resolution that passed was a weak legislative tool, expressing only the sense of the Senate and not possessing the force of law.

Beginning in 1966, there was growing agitation to bring at least some portion of these troops home. This agitation had several causes: the Vietnam-induced disillusionment with the efficacy of military forces; the French withdrawal from the military side of NATO and a sense that the United States was doing more than its fair share; and, as time went on, the declining value of the dollar relative to the German mark, which made it more expensive to maintain the troops in the NATO area.[11]

Senator Mike Mansfield (D-Montana) became the leading spokesman for efforts to reduce troop strength in Europe. Annually, from 1966 to 1971, Senator Mansfield introduced a sense of the Senate resolution that American forces in Europe should be reduced. The series of resolutions had little impact; but in 1971, Senator Mansfield changed his strategy and proposed an amendment to the selective service bill that would limit funds to the amount necessary to support 150,000 troops—essentially mandating a reduction in troop strength of 50 percent. Mansfield's amendment was not successful, but it did provoke a major debate in the Senate over the issue of the appropriate level and kind of support the United States was providing the NATO alliance.

In recent years, the issue of U.S. troop strength in Europe has emerged again as a subject for discussion. In 1984, Senators Sam Nunn (D-Georgia) and William Cohen (Rep.-Maine) proposed to reduce the level of U.S. troops in Europe unless the Europeans moved to improve their defense capabilities.[12] The United States still maintains the equivalent of five divisions in Europe—4 Army divisions, 2 separate brigades, 2 armored cavalry regiments, and 28 air force squadrons—for a force within NATO second in size and combat capability only to the West German *Bundeswehr*.

Intermediate Range Nuclear Forces. During the late 1970s, European leaders, perceiving the buildup in Soviet weaponry and the Carter Administration's eagerness to reach agreement with the Soviets on SALT, began to fear a disassociation of U.S. security interests from Western Europe. The emergence of new ground-based weapons technologies, in particular cruise missiles, provided a mechanism for the forging of stronger links in the deterrence chain and a coupling of U.S. and European security interests. The 1979 two-track decision on Intermediate Range Nuclear Forces (INF), coupling modernization with arms control, was the result of these developments. The question of positioning American intermediate range nuclear weapons in Europe in response to Soviet fielding of the SS-20 has undoubtedly generated the most heat of any issue that has challenged the alliance. From the perspective of this analysis, what is most interesting is that two major players, Germany and the United States, have essentially exchanged positions on this issue between the first discussions of INF modernization and the present time.

Initially, Germany was in favor of positioning Pershing II and GLCM in Europe; in the sunny days of detente, the Germans feared superpower condominium and the sacrifice of Western Europe. The United States was initially lukewarm to the idea, principally because of President Carter's quest for arms control and his personal stake in SALT II. Both nations, however, soon changed positions as a result of internal political developments. The U.S. effort to field enhanced-radiation weapons in Europe gave impetus to the antinuclear movement in Germany, which soon focused on the to-be-deployed Pershing II and GLCM. In the United States, domestic suspicion of arms control, mistrust of the Soviets, and a general recognition as post-Vietnam antimilitarism waned that U.S. forces had been allowed to deteriorate led to support for increases in INF deployments in Europe.[13]

Strategic Defense Initiative. The most dramatic change in the focus of U.S. defense policy in the postwar era was initiated by President Reagan in his now-famous speech of March 23, 1983, in which he proposed the development of a system of strategic defense against ballistic missiles. He took most strategic analysts by surprise when he included in his speech his suggestion for ballistic missile defense development efforts; most people thought the ABM debate had been quietly put to bed in the early 1970s. Not surprisingly, he took most members of Congress by surprise as well. They had to scramble to begin to understand an extremely complex set of technical issues, interweave them with a level of understanding of U.S. policy and strategy toward the world, and emerge with a position for or against the Strategic Defense Initiative (SDI), as it was called by its supporters, or "Star Wars," as it was indelibly christened by Senator Edward Kennedy.

The pro- and anti-SDI factions began to form on Capitol Hill, following party lines to some extent, although there was and continues to be substantial crossover. For each of the first three budget cycles for which SDI funds occupied discrete line items, Congress refused to give the administration what it wanted for SDI (although it still gave it billions of dollars in one of the fastest ramp-ups in defense program history). For the first two years of identifiable SDI program funding

(1984 and 1985), the role of Congress in the development of SDI was an examiner (and usually cutter) of budgets.

Surrounding the development of the FY 86 Department of Defense budget for SDI, however, there began to emerge some policy-oriented discussion that suggests the future involvement of the Congress in SDI may be more substantive than budgetary. From the inception of the program, the broadest definition of the Strategic Defense Initiative included the defense of Western Europe. In its initial phases, however, much of the SDI-related discussion focused on either terminal defenses of military installations or space-based exotic weapons to counter the threat from ICBMs; Europe once again began to feel decoupled from the U.S. nuclear umbrella and feared a potential negative effect on deterrence.

In recognition of this uneasiness, the administration in the spring of 1985 called for increased attention to alliance participation in SDI. By the end of 1985, an agreement had been reached on British participation in SDI, and discussions with West Germany and Italy were well advanced. Clearly, the administration recognized both the military and the political need to ensure the recognition that SDI was part of the fabric of alliance policy, not simply a U.S. initiative.

As the administration pursued efforts to involve the NATO allies in the business of SDI, the Congress began to examine the implications of such involvement for things like property rights, commercial spinoffs, security standards, and other matters. The Senate agreed to an amendment to the FY 86 defense spending bill that would prevent the Pentagon from establishing special funds to be set aside for foreign contractors. In addition, Rep. Les Aspin (D-Wisconsin), Chairman of the House Armed Services Committee, wrote to Defense Secretary Weinberger seeking answers to questions on topics such as funding mechanisms for cooperative participation in SDI, technology transfer terms, property rights, and competition. At the time of this writing, the shape of ultimate NATO participation in SDI was not clear; what was clear, however, was that the Congress intended to ensure that the administration did not "buy support" for SDI internationally by assuring the allies a piece of the action.[14]

A final factor complicating the involvement of the European NATO allies in SDI is the emergence of some pressure for the development of a European counterpart to SDI, focused on defense against shorter range ballistic and nonballistic tactical nuclear missiles, including cruise missiles. Whether the European members of NATO will try to establish a separate program to accommodate their own defense needs, or try to piggyback on the SDI, is still uncertain as of this writing. Either way, Congress will have something to say about it.

INFLUENCES ON WHAT CONGRESS DOES

The preceding section provides some examples of issues directly affecting the NATO alliance in which the Congress has played a visible, significant role. The evidence presented solidifies the assertion made earlier that Congress acts, not on the basis of functional imperatives generated in the international environment, but on the basis of domestic constraints arising from the political culture and circumstances of the nation. Political pressures to remove troops from Europe were generated by perceptions that the United States was carrying more than its fair share of the defense burden of the alliance, not by assumptions that the threat no longer called for U.S. troops in Europe. The positioning of Pershing II and GLCM in Europe was driven more by political pressures from a public that no longer wanted to be perceived as international patsies than by perceptions of the threat; after all, Pershing II and GLCM could do nothing to defend against the SS-20s deployed in the Soviet Union, and the needs of deterrence were met by SLBM and ICBM forces. And finally, the questions that have begun to emerge relative to European participation in the Strategic Defense Initiative revolve around the threat to U.S. industry, not the threat to either the United States or Europe posed by the Soviet Union.

The pressures of geography and history that affect the way nations react to international events have already been discussed. Congress, as part of American society, is not immune from these generalized pressures. But Congress, as a political institution, is affected by some very specific factors of domestic politics through which the general political cultural biases are played out.[15] Future Congressional attitudes toward NATO are likely to be driven by these factors; they therefore bear examination.

Macroeconomic Considerations

There is no question that government spending stimulates the economy—and defense spending has that effect. It is important to come to an understanding of the relative impact of defense spending as compared to spending in other sectors of the economy. There are experts and data on both sides of the question. On the one hand, the capital-intensive nature of defense spending makes it a greater economic multiplier than other government spending. On the other hand, the high skill requirements and high salaries demanded by the jobs created by defense spending minimizes its impact on hard-core unemployment. One study showed that, per dollar, military expenditures generate half as many jobs, but 20 percent more salary dollars than civilian expenditures.[16] Arthur Burns, former chairman of the Federal Reserve, reflected the prevailing uncertainty over the macroeconomic effects of defense spending when he stated: "If the defense sector has stimulated economic growth in some directions, it has retarded growth in others."[17]

Spending specifically for NATO complicates these effects in two ways. First, members of the military stationed in Europe spend their money in Europe rather than America; to the extent that this money is spent off-post, it contributes to the economic well-being of Europe rather than the United States. Second, to whatever extent NATO systems are codeveloped or coproduced with European industrial partners, the contribution to American industrial development and GNP diminishes. Compared with the other factors that influence the attitudes of Congress toward NATO, only the latter is likely to have any significant impact, and that will be felt more in the SDI program than anyplace else.

Federal Budget and Fiscal Policies

There are two components to this factor: the guns/butter tradeoff and the problem of Federal deficits.

Guns vs. Butter. Defense programs are seen as a direct competitor for increasingly scarce resources with domestic social programs. It is common to hear statements about how many poor people could be fed for the cost of one C5-A, for example. When the money being spent on defense programs is earmarked for the defense of Europe, while Americans are subjected to the sight and sound of anti-American demonstrations and continue to hear from our Congressmen that Europe is spending a substantially lesser proportion of its GNP for defense than the United States is, the impetus to withdraw from Europe and spend U.S. dollars to meet our U.S. domestic needs is strong. The European allies do not really understand this controversy. According to one observer,

> While the United States continues to debate seriously the relative importance of spending for social welfare as compared to spending for defense, this issue was settled a century ago in Europe. Sacrificing social welfare for defense spending in any situation short of war itself simply lacks a European constituency. Social welfare is fully integrated into what Western Europe understands liberal democracy to mean.[18]

Federal Budget Deficit. The Federal budget deficit is increasingly a subject of concern in the Congress and across the country. The Gramm-Rudman-Hollings deficit reduction bill that passed Congress in the fall of 1985 is one Congressional initiative that forced a recognition that all government programs—including defense—face reduction to address the deficit. Several compromises were reached in the course of debate over Gramm-Rudman that will mitigate the bill's effects on defense, at least initially: existing government contracts are exempted by the bill; for the first year (FY 86) the Defense Department will be able to pick and choose which programs it wants to cut and by how much; and the Defense Department has found over $6 billion in authorized and appropriated but unspent funds that it expects to use to offset cuts that it does incur. Beginning in FY 87, however, all eligible programs will be cut across the board by whatever amount necessary to balance the budget, unless they fall under the category deemed critical. Such programs are likely to be the big-ticket, strategic programs; there is speculation that conventional weapons programs will suffer the most under Gramm-Rudman. Since these programs are targeted largely on the defense of Europe, it is likely that spending on NATO-related concerns will take a disproportionate hit under Gramm-Rudman. At this writing, the constitutional and legislative challenges being levied against the mechanisms of the Gramm-Rudman law are still unresolved. But regardless of the fate of Gramm-Rudman, it is clear that the United States is entering an era of concern over the magnitude of Federal deficits. Over the next several years, budgets will be cut, and spending for NATO concerns will not be immune from cuts.

Internal Defense Budget Issues

There are two components to this factor as well: interservice rivalry and defense procurement reform.

Interservice Rivalry. In the early spring of each year, the services begin a series of visits to Capitol Hill to argue for their piece of the defense budget. There is a sophisticated gamesmanship that goes on during this process: everyone knows the defense budget is going to be cut, and each service stands to gain or lose prestige by the extent to which its budget stays intact. Although the budget discussions are focused on programs, the end result has strategic implications, because each service has a specific mission to fill. If one service wins out over another, its mission becomes more prominent and strategy is influenced, at least at the margins.

The importance of this for NATO is that the bulk of U.S. expenditures for NATO go to the ground forces, and this means the Army. In recent years, we have seen the Navy achieve great success in garnering for itself a larger share of the defense budget on its way to reaching its goal of a 600-ship fleet. Conventional ground forces for Europe and elsewhere have suffered by comparison. Even more recently, during 1984 and 1985 we saw the emergence of a major new focus for defense spending—the Strategic Defense Initiative. As the services wrangle for a share of this pot, conventional defense in Europe might again find itself on the back burner.

Defense Procurement Policy Reform. Much of the debate over the FY 86 defense budget focused on various suggestions for reforming the way the defense department conducted business with the private sector. For years, tales of waste, mismanagement, and outright fraud in the defense procurement process had been the focus of media attention. The overall trend in the various suggestions for reform that accompanied the FY 86 budget debates was to encourage competition in defense industry—reducing the reliance on sole-source contracts and requiring competition for major procurements. The impact of these efforts on the defense procurement process in general is indeterminant— for one reason, because most of the reform suggestions were eliminated from the budget legislation through the compromises exacted in the conference committee. However, the impetus is still there for procurement reform. This has the potential to affect NATO in that the services are increasingly being asked to look to European companies to provide additional competition for hardware and services normally provided to the government by private industry. The competition generated by these government initiatives involves increasingly complex contract award decisions. It also places European companies in the position of competing with U.S. firms for business, rather than developing complementary capabilities as encouraged by the longstanding emphasis on rationalization of the NATO weapons development process.

Public Opinion

Elsewhere in this volume, Gregory Foster has discussed public opinion and the alliance at some length. Nonetheless, it needs to be considered here as one of the domestic factors to which Congress must be responsive. The easiest way to understand the influence of public opinion on Congressional action is to reflect on the thesis of *Congress: The Electoral Connection*, by David R. Mayhew.[19] The essential argument of this book is that the primary function of a Congressman is to be reelected—that it is from the electoral imperative that the richest understanding of the factors that motivate Congressional actions can be drawn. The problem with this perspective lies in the fact that public opinion as it affects the way people vote is diverse, difficult to assess, and more than occasionally an ill-informed guide to the best interests of the republic. Still, Congressmen and Senators pay a great deal of attention to public opinion as they can discern it, through the media and through attention to expressions of interest from their constituencies.

Public opinion as it relates to defense issues is a complicated phenomenon. Americans hold a generally ambivalent attitude toward their military institutions. They are heir to a powerful antimilitary tradition, yet they are willing to support participation in conflict if they feel threatened. They tend to ignore the military until they need it, at which time they expect it to rise to the occasion and keep them secure. Most rational Americans understand the need to support forces in peacetime if they are to be ready for war, but the strategy of deterrence imposes a greater obligation on an informed population. Deterrence requires that the people be willing to support forces in peacetime, not in anticipation of their eventual use in wartime, but so that they will never be used. The illogic of deterrence, coupled with what appears to be an element of fundamental irrationality in nuclear policy, confuses public opinion. As Lawrence Freedman put it, "The attempt to deter conventional aggression in Europe with a nuclear arsenal controlled by a non-European power that is itself subject to nuclear retaliation has never appeared to be an example of political or military rationality."[20]

At the same time that the difficulty in understanding strategy was growing, it was becoming increasingly less likely that civilians would be able to avoid being directly impacted by warfare. A common scenario for nuclear war involves at least the possibility of strikes against civilian population centers (the countervalue option); casualties among noncombatants behind the front line would be higher than those among troops on the line. This realization has led large numbers of citizens to try to understand the intricacies of nuclear policy; greater popular attention to issues of nuclear policy have revealed its bizarre nature and further undermined trust in the defense establishment.

In addition, the shocks of the 1970s—Iran, Afghanistan, OPEC and the related oil crisis, the Soviet buildup—led Americans to feel that they had lost control of their domestic and international environments. Among other things, it became difficult to forge a consensus behind policies that involve compromise, subtlety, patience, restraint, prior consultation with allies, and the geopolitical maneuvering required when one is no longer the focus of world military and economic power.[21] This was made quite clear by one observer who noted that:

> Our citizens understood the Great Crusade from 1941–1945, and the clear outcome was gratifying, but since then both clarity and gratification have been denied us. Impatience with ambiguity characterizes the American popular mood of the early 1980s, and strategists are almost as confused as the people while the sorting out of priorities takes place. One of the issues requiring hard thought is the place of our security arrangement with Europe and how it fits into an emerging global strategy.[22]

Another analyst put it more bluntly:

(The defense of NATO) involves so many bizarre issues, especially when tactical nuclear weapons are brought into the picture, that any analysis of the problem in peacetime takes on an aura of either sterility or surrealism. . . . The NATO defense problem is discussed in terms of an abstract exchange of weapons between two missile farms that happen to have countries attached to them.[23]

SUMMARY AND CONCLUSIONS

The enduring political problems of the NATO alliance are not signs of the alliance's impending demise, but of the diverse nature of its membership. In particular, the differences in perceptions held by the United States and the major European members of the alliance are the source of much of the turmoil in NATO. The differences in perceptions stems from the long-term geographic and historical circumstances that influence each nation's political culture. This factor is driven home by Henry Gole, who concludes that we are in Europe, not to protect the Europeans, but to protect our own interests:

Indignant, even incredulous, American voices have been asking why the United States should be more concerned with European security than Europeans seem to be. The question misses the point on two counts: first, we aren't; we're concerned with U.S. security; second, Europeans are concerned but can't do much more about their security position without risking the transformation of the very natures of their societies or possibly making the problem worse by enraging the bear.[24]

Mancur Olson's theory of collective action helps to dispel some of the confusion surrounding the contributions to collective defense made by each member of the alliance. In Olson's terms, a rational member of the alliance would sit back and let the United States provide the benefits of alliance—would be a "free rider"—because once the United States has provided for its own security it has gone a long way toward providing for the security of Europe. The United States feels exploited by the "free rider" mentality it sees in the European members of the alliance because it perceives European interests to be virtually identical to U.S. interests.

The Europeans, however, feel that their interests are not identical to U.S. interests: the United States views Europe as "theater" and has other global interests that contend with Europe; the United States talks about the military utility of nuclear weapons, whereas Europe sees them as useful only as a deterrent; Americans see the struggle with the Soviet Union as an ultimate struggle of good versus evil, whereas Europeans, with a longer historical view, take a more relaxed approach to yet another effort to achieve hegemony over the continent. Perhaps at root it is the European minimalist approach to NATO strategy that exasperates American leaders and causes them to charge Europe with attempting to get a free ride.[25]

Europeans, however, reject the idea that they are getting a free ride, pointing to the fact that the European allies contribute 90 percent of the land forces and 80 percent of the aircraft fielded by NATO. In their eyes, they are doing their fair share. The political problems of the alliance do not arise because interests of member nations are too diverse. These problems occur because they are close enough that those areas where they do diverge are thrown into high relief, and Americans, who perceive that it is the American nuclear umbrella that makes the alliance work, want to see divergent opinions resolved in America's favor.

NOTES

1. Samuel P. Huntington, *The Soldier and the State* (New York: Random House, 1957).

2. Henry G. Gole, "NATO Defense Through European Eyes," in Robert Kennedy and John M. Weinstein, eds. *The Defense of the West* (Boulder, CO: Westview Press, 1984), p. 420.

3. Gole, "NATO Defense Through European Eyes," p. 418.

4. William Bader, "Congress and the Making of U.S. Security Policies," in *American Security in the 1980s (Adelphi Papers No. 173)* (International Institute of Strategic Studies, 1982), p. 14.

5. Quoted on the cover of *Armed Forces Journal International* (March 1986).

6. Thomas A. Callaghan, Jr., "New Treaty of Technology and Trade," in Kenneth A. Myers' *NATO: The Next Thirty Years* (Boulder, CO: Westview Press, 1980), p. 299.

7. Callaghan, "New Treaty of Technology and Trade," p. 300.

8. Quoted in Cecil V. Crabb, Jr. and Pat M. Holt, *Invitation to Struggle: Congress, the President, and Foreign Policy* (Washington, DC: Congressional Quarterly Press, 1980), p. 121. The ungrammatical character of the quotation is the original text.

9. *Ibid.*, p. 121.

10. *Ibid.*, p. 121.

11. *Ibid.*, p. 122.

12. James A. Thomson and Nanette C. Brown, "Theater Forces: U.S. Defense Policy in NATO," in George E. Hudson and Joseph Kruzel, *American Defense Annual 1985-1986* (Lexington, MA: D. C. Heath and Company, 1985), p. 98.

13. Josef Joffe, "Allies, Angst, and Arms Control: New Troubles for an Old Partnership," in Marsha McGrew Olive and Jeffrey D. Porro, *Nuclear Weapons in Europe* (Lexington, MA: D. C. Heath and Company, 1983), pp. 26–27.

14. *Defense News* (December 16, 1985), p. 2.

15. Philip Odeen, "Domestic Factors in U.S. Defense Policy," in *American Security in the 1980s (Adelphi Papers No. 173)* (International Institute of Strategic Studies, 1982), p. 22.

16. Jacques Gansler, *The Defense Industry* (Cambridge, MA: MIT Press, 1980), p. 14.

17. *Ibid.*, p. 14.

18. Gole, "NATO Defense Through European Eyes," p. 420.

19. David R. Mayhew, *Congress: The Electoral Connection* (New Haven: Yale University Press, 1974).

20. Lawrence Freedman, "NATO Myths," *Foreign Policy*, No. 45 (Winter 1981–82), p. 50.

21. Odeen, "Domestic Factors in U.S. Defense Policy," p. 28.

22. Gole, "NATO Defense Through European Eyes," p. 414.

23. Paul Bracken, "The NATO Defense Problem," *Orbis* (Spring 1983), p. 83.

24. Gole, "NATO Defense Through European Eyes," p. 419.

25. *Ibid.*, p. 429.

5

PUBLIC OPINION: THE FULCRUM OF ALLIANCE COHESION

Gregory D. Foster

By commonly acknowledged principles of general alliance theory, NATO as a viable and enduring pact is an anachronism. In one especially illuminating and scholarly treatment of the subject, Alan Ned Sabrosky has suggested that the *least* reliable alliances are multilateral pacts with signatories differing greatly in power, political regime, and proportional contributions to the alliance, who had undertaken to provide unspecified (or unlimited) assistance to one another for an indefinite period of time, in light of an alleged moral obligation or ideological bond.[1] NATO comes perilously close to fulfilling all of these criteria.

Such considerations, as well as many others of a less scholarly, more visceral nature, have prompted a wave of "nouveau chic" criticism of NATO as an alliance "uncertain," "adrift," or "in crisis."[2] Even such incongruous ideological soulmates as Richard Barnet and Irving Kristol have observed respectively that "the NATO allies are drifting apart," and "the Atlantic Alliance . . . is gradually emptying itself of all meaning."[3]

Others—most notably Earl Ravenal—have argued that, in the interest of "the economy of alliance," the United States should disengage itself from NATO. Ravenal argues that the commitment to Europe presents the United States with a choice between high, and perhaps unsupportable, costs associated with the confident conventional defense of Europe, and unassumable risks attributable to reliance on the earlier use of nuclear weapons. A thorough and consistent disengagement would shed both the responsibilities and the burdens of alliance.[4]

In the course of developing this argument, Ravenal acknowledges that the crises which periodically confront NATO are not random; they are all tests of confidence among the allies. The crises also are neither accidental nor superficial; they derive from deep causal roots—divergent conceptions of alliance, divergent security needs, and the divergent geopolitical situations of America and Europe. Finally, these crises are not novel; they stem from problems that have been implicit in the alliance from its inception.[5]

The true import of these insights, compellingly stated as they are, is the implicit recognition that the issues which have bedeviled NATO over the years—burden-sharing, the so-called "one-way street" of arms cooperation, out-of-theater crises, neutralism and global unilateralism, etc.—have been, at root, perceptual rather than structural questions concerning the commitment, the intentions, and the motives of alliance partners. In other words, the solidarity of an alliance—NATO or any other—revolves ultimately around what is in the minds of the various parties to the partnership rather than around the more mechanistic aspects of how the alliance is organized or what procedures it follows.

Alliance cohesion is a phenomenon of more than passing interest to scholars and practitioners alike—much discussed, but seemingly little understood.[6] Regrettably, its relationship to public opinion has not been explored in any depth; yet there is a sufficiently compelling intuitive basis for arguing that public opinion actually may be the "fulcrum" of alliance cohesion. Upon it, precariously balanced, rests the continuum of thought and action that reflects the alliance's propensities toward integration: from cohesion, born of bona fide internal consensus, at the one extreme, to the negation of cohesion—disintegration, born of total dissensus—at the other extreme. Fuller exploration of this argument in the NATO context requires, at the outset, that we come to grips with two fundamental questions:

- First, are there compelling reasons, contrary to the naysayers, why the cohesion of the NATO alliance is, and should be, an intrinsically important objective in its own right?
- Second, what is the ultimate source of U.S. disaffection with the alliance, and is it of such deep-seated significance as to impede future efforts at maintaining cohesion and performance?

WHY MAINTAIN THE ALLIANCE?

Most arguments put forth to date for the dissolution of, or American withdrawal from, NATO are based, at least implicitly, on the premises that (a) an alliance is merely a means to an end, and (b) either the end does not justify the means or the end is better served by other means. There are, however, strong arguments in favor of maintaining NATO and America's role in that alliance that are based on the belief that to do so is a worthwhile end in itself. The first of these arguments—what George Quester has characterized as the "American liberal" perspective—is that we are bound to Europe by philosophical values, and by ties of culture and heritage. Although we readily acknowledge that Europe has been a "liability," an "entangling commitment," it is a commitment valued for its own sake rather than as a means to ends anywhere else on the globe.[7]

A second argument, put forth by Michael Howard, is that the American military presence is necessary not only in the negative sense as a *deterrent* to Soviet aggression, but also in the positive sense of *reassurance* to the Western Europeans. The reconciliation of these two imperatives—to persuade the Soviet Union that the costs of seeking a military solution to its political problems will far outweigh the benefits, and to persuade our own people, and those of our allies, that the benefits of military action, or preparation for it, will outweigh the costs—is basic to the creation of consensus within the alliance. The reassurance on which most Europeans rely, says Howard, is the presence among them of American troops.[8]

A third reason for maintaining the alliance has been offered by Josef Joffe, who argues that without the United States, Western Europe might revert to the pattern of interaction that characterized the period prior to World War II rather than surge forward toward true integration. The weak states would once more worry about the strong, and the strong—such as Great Britain, France, and West Germany—would once more worry about one another. This would prompt the Soviet Union to use its overweening strength to play one state against another and to dictate the terms of its relationship to them all. West Germany, in turn, would arm itself with nuclear weapons, and others in the region would follow suit. Joffe points out the curious twist this offers to alliance theory. Whereas conventional theory holds that states coalesce in order to assure their security, the NATO states coalesced because their security was assured—by a powerful outsider (the United States) that delivered both external protection and internal order. Order thus was the precondition of alliance and integration.[9]

Robert Tucker has provided yet another rationale—less in support of his own position on the issue than as an acknowledgment of extant realities. Tucker's contention is that one consequence of our displacement from NATO would be the need to make a substantially greater defense effort than we currently are making, *if* we were to maintain our position elsewhere in the world. This is contrary to the prevailing logic of critics such as Ravenal. If we were to withdraw from Europe, and the West Europeans failed to fill the gap, the Soviet Union would have much less to worry about in the theater of greatest importance to it. Freed of this concern, and strengthened by the resource base of Western Europe, Moscow could turn its full attention elsewhere. Thus, rather than closing the gap between our commitments and our power, Soviet ascendance in Europe following American withdrawal actually could widen the gap.[10]

More than any of these arguments, though, the most convincing rationale for seeking to maintain the NATO alliance in its present form is to provide a direct counter to Soviet strategy. The intrinsic value of this objective is found in the principle enunciated over 2000 years ago by Chinese scholar Sun Tzu, who suggested that "what is of supreme importance in war is to attack the enemy's strategy."[11]

Today, after some four decades of experience, there is a slowly growing recognition that the basic Soviet strategy in Europe is, in the words of U.S. Ambassador to NATO, David Abshire, "to split the alliance and separate the United States from Europe."[12] Edward Luttwak, in his study of Soviet grand strategy, similarly has noted that the central goal of the Kremlin's foreign policy throughout the postwar era has been to erode and if possible break the security nexus between the United States and Western Europe. To accomplish this, the Soviets have employed the entire panoply of instruments of statecraft available to them—from the softest kind of allusive diplomacy to outright threats, from the general buildup of military power to the manipulation of trade links with Western Europe.[13]

Numerous other authorities have echoed this position.[14] The true sophistication of the Soviet strategy has been captured by Coit Dennis Blacker, who argues that Moscow's objective clearly is to ease the United States out of Europe in stages, while at the same time seeking to dissuade the NATO allies from rushing in to fill the vacuum. By simultaneously, but independently, cultivating better relations with the United States and the Western European countries, by quietly exploiting the latent and not-so-latent tensions that exist among the Atlantic states, and by pursuing a policy of moderation that encourages fragmentation rather than consolidation within the West, the Soviets can anticipate a gradual and uneven weakening of the bonds that link Washington to NATO Europe.[15]

It is within this context and based on recognition of such conditions that former President Richard Nixon has averred that we have been engaged in World War III since the closing days of World War II. It is, in Nixon's words, the first truly total war we have experienced, waged on all levels of life and society.[16] Hyperbolic and somewhat paranoid though this assessment may seem, it is a perspective that remains largely beyond the ken of most Americans to grasp. The ingrained American aversion to war tends to cloud our perception of conflict and its many dimensions—violence commonly being adjudged the central defining characteristic of conflict and thus to be assiduously avoided.

Whereas the United States, as a power basically interested in preserving the international status quo, regards peace as the absence of war, the Soviet Union, as a power interested in changing the international status quo, believes that peace is impossible so long as there remain all those conditions of exploitation and oppression which produce class struggle. Whatever outsiders may say in rejection of the seemingly hackneyed and overdrawn arguments of some commentators concerning the pervasiveness of Marxist-Leninist ideology in contemporary Soviet thought, there is no denying the legacy of intellectual inculcation that remains. The "struggle between the two social systems" of capitalism and communism is an institutionalized belief that suffuses the Soviet world view. Certainly this must be said to be so among the Russian elite, whose price of ascension to power has been defined in such ideological coinage.[17]

We see in Soviet strategy the thinking of Clausewitz to be sure: his emphasis on the inextricable link between war and politics; the critical importance of surprise and its concomitant, deception; and the necessity of identifying and striking at the enemy's center of gravity. More significant than the influence of Clausewitz on Soviet strategy, though, has been the influence of Sun Tzu. Whereas to Clausewitz war was an act of physical force which manifests itself in combat with the enemy, to Sun Tzu war was best fought not on the battlefield but in the preceding peacetime. The object is not the use of military violence, but the undermining of the legitimacy of the opponent's cause among his own people. Legitimacy is the key concept—the quest for the hearts and minds of the other party's population. Victory comes when extraordinary, or indirect, force is married with direct force. Extraordinary force—spreading false rumors, corrupting officials, creating internal discord, and nurturing fifth columns—is applied extensively to weaken an opponent to the point where only a minimum of ordinary force is required to topple him. Such precepts were not lost on Lenin, who himself observed: "The soundest strategy is to postpone operations until the moral disintegration of the enemy renders the delivery of the mortal blow both possible and easy."[18]

The political struggle against capitalism has been described by some Soviet commentators as "the struggle for the minds and hearts of people throughout the world." There is explicit recognition in the Soviet literature of the increasing role of the masses in the making of foreign policy. Georgi Arbatov of the Institute for the U.S.A. and Canada, for example, contends that it is impossible for governments to be successful unless they effectively communicate their policies and actions to all politically influential segments of foreign populations, as well as to the domestic population. Thus, he suggests, there now exists a "diplomacy of public opinion," involving an even more pronounced emphasis on ideology and propaganda than in the past. For this reason, the Soviets see the monopoly of modern means of mass communication as being no less important than the monopoly of traditional instruments of power.[19]

In their important study of the subject, *Dezinformatsia*, Richard H. Shultz and Roy Godson present a convincing picture of how the Soviets have made extensive use of so-called "active measures"—propaganda, disinformation, forgeries, agents of influence, front groups, etc.—as an integral part of their overall strategy to weaken the United States and NATO. Active measures regularly are employed to influence the policies of other governments, to undermine public confidence in the leaders and institutions of those governments, to disrupt relations between other nations, and to discredit and weaken governmental and non-governmental opponents. Available evidence suggests that Soviet leaders have sought, through the use of active measures, to achieve a number of specific aims, including the following:

- To influence American, European, and world public opinion to believe that U.S. military and political policies are the major cause of international conflict and crisis.
- To isolate the United States from its friends and allies (especially those in NATO), and to discredit those states which cooperate with the United States.
- To discredit the U.S. and NATO military and intelligence establishments.[20]

Soviet active measures have, in the words of former Under Secretary of State Lawrence Eagleburger, exerted a corrosive effect on Western political systems. The confusions produced by media manipulations, forgeries, calculated rumors, falsely attributed radio broadcasts, and the activities of agents of influence may, over time, Eagleburger believes, weaken public confidence in political institutions and processes.[21]

Additionally, active Soviet support of emerging European peace movements seems designed to further Moscow's perceived security needs by promoting instability among Western nations. The hope of Soviet leaders, it has been suggested, is that the wide cross-section of

Western public opinion dedicated to the preservation of peace will, through participation in the antiwar movement, eventually become sufficiently radicalized and alienated from their elected governments as to become, if not "revolutionary," or "anticapitalist," then at least neutralist and anti-American.[22]

The battle being waged in Europe today is taking place not on the battlefields of the continent but in the hearts and minds of the European populace. By engaging in the concurrent pursuit of intimidation and moral suasion, the Soviets are playing on the type of intellectual ambiguity most difficult for Western minds to grasp. By focusing on issues of peace and war, they are exploiting the precarious balance between emotion and rationality that, if properly manipulated, can create wide cleavages even among seemingly like-minded peoples. By targeting mass audiences and exploiting modern communications techniques, they are evincing an appreciation of contemporary realities—rising expectations fed by growing popular awareness; acute frustration with the performance of governing elites; and the diffusion of power to multiple publics. Most importantly, by employing such methods, the Soviets are seeking to accomplish without force what their innate sense of insecurity and aversion to risk will not let them attempt with force—even if we are too obtuse to recognize this characteristic pattern of bullying behavior.

The sophistication of Soviet strategy in Europe should be a lesson to Western strategists and an object of special concern to bureaucratically minded decisionmakers. Even though—as the most knowledgeable Soviet watchers among us would be quick to point out—Moscow's methods frequently have been crude, its approach has been sound. The game at hand is a rather masterful exercise in strategic indirection that would make even the late B. H. Liddell Hart beam with admiration. Thus, even if there were no other convincing reasons for maintaining the integrity of the NATO alliance, the defeat of Soviet strategy alone would provide a compelling rationale for doing so. If we are to thwart Soviet designs, however, we must engage in some critical self-appraisal to determine whether we are intellectually equipped to fight fire with fire. This brings us to the second of the two questions posed at the outset of this discussion.

THE FRUSTRATIONS OF DEMOCRACY

U.S. ability to respond to the situation in Europe suffers perhaps more than anything from the internal contradictions of our own attitude toward democracy in the alliance context. This reflects deep underlying shortcomings in our general conception of democracy, as well as a latent authoritarian view of America's proper role in the alliance. Our relationship to our NATO allies today is not unlike that of the parent who painfully resists relinquishing dominance over his children, but who is forced to concede, in the interest of family unity, that the children have grown up and earned their independence. The weakness of such an analogy, of course, is that whereas unity is an expectable goal in the family context, harmony may be the more realistic goal within an alliance of nations.

According to Robert Dahl, an ideal democratic process would satisfy five criteria:

1. Equality in voting: In making collective binding decisions, the expressed preference of each citizen ought to be taken equally into account in determining the final solution.
2. Effective participation: Throughout the process of collective decisionmaking, including the stage of putting matters on the agenda, each citizen ought to have adequate and equal opportunities for expressing his or her preferences as to the final outcome.
3. Enlightened understanding: In the time permitted by the need for a decision, each citizen ought to have adequate and equal opportunities for arriving at his or her considered judgment as to the most desirable outcome.
4. Final control over the agenda: The body of citizens (the demos) should have the exclusive authority to determine what matters are or are not to be decided by means of processes that satisfy the first three criteria.
5. Inclusion: The demos ought to include all adults subject to its laws, except transients.[23]

As Dahl is quick to point out, the ideal criteria are so demanding that no actual regime has ever fully met them. Possibly none ever will.[24] The United States never has attained this pinnacle, primarily because we as a nation have adhered theoretically to a standard that more closely approximates republican majoritarianism than the democratic ideal. Among the Founding Fathers, it was Jefferson who set the tone: "The first principle of republicanism is, that the lex majoris partis is the fundamental law of every society of individuals of equal rights. . . ." But Lincoln stated it most succinctly: "Unanimity is impossible; the rule of a minority, as a permanent arrangement, is wholly inadmissible; so that, rejecting the majority principle, anarchy or despotism in some form is all that is left."[25]

Juxtaposed against this prevailing conception has been our own practice of hybrid democracy in which, as Dahl also notes, on matters of specific policy the majority rarely rules.[26] This basic fact has been elevated to its highest form in the international arena, where sovereign actors of every size and persuasion aggressively compete for recognition and bargaining power. That we have been so impatient, frustrated, and disaffected with supranational enterprises of any stripe is directly attributable not only to our inherited republican impulses but also to our resolute adherence to a Wilsonian paradigm of governance, key elements of which include the following:

- That there will always be a single dominant center of power in any system of government;
- That the more power is divided, the more irresponsible it becomes; and,
- That the perfection of "good" administration (defined as the maximization of efficiency) is a necessary condition for modernity in human civilization and for the advancement of human welfare.[27]

Thus, our standard for judging performance at the supranational level has been efficiency, a criterion that dooms us to self-assessed failure. NATO, accordingly, may be characterized as an exercise in "meta-democracy," an intermediate step between the parochial model of the independent nation-state and the failed experiences of the League of Nations, the United Nations, and other less ambitious attempts at sustained, institutionalized, cooperative multinational endeavors. Those who would have us withdraw from NATO are admitting—albeit inadvertently—their distaste for the practical aspects of democracy and their preference for efficiency as an ideal. Conversely, those who would go to the other extreme and advocate an expanded "alliance of democracies" betray a degree of naivete—perhaps even hypocrisy—in their judgments of who we are and what we stand for in our practical dealings with friends abroad.[28]

The case can be made that certain latent, largely unrecognized, features of the American character actually may be terminal impediments to the maintenance of cohesion within the Atlantic alliance. If true, this presents us with an acute dilemma, for even as we must acknowledge the intrinsic importance of ensuring the integrity of the alliance, so too must we concede that our own ingrained values and biases may have an insidious effect on our ability to achieve such a goal. The problem is compounded by the fact that its underlying causes are not endemic to the United States and thus not amenable to correction by our actions alone. There are, in fact, pervasive forces at work in the contemporary international environment that make the problem seem almost intractable.

The first of these forces, admittedly speculative in nature, is what one observer of the American scene has termed the Law of Inversely Proportional Stupidity.[29] The "law" states that there is an inverse correlation between the civilizational progress of a society and the logical thinking capability of its members; the higher the level of science and technology, the lower the understanding of interhuman relations. In other words, the more advanced a society the less able its leaders are to interpret broader social and political developments accurately. In the alliance context, this suggests that as we and our allies continue to advance scientifically, technologically, and presumably economically, our tendency will be to accept such achievements as measures of fundamental progress while blinding us ever more to the human dynamics that ultimately will determine the future of the alliance.

A second, related force at work in the contemporary international environment is the fragmenting effect of technology. In contrast to the mass society and global village once envisioned by media guru Marshall McLuhan, technology today seems actually to have produced a trend toward the fragmentation of society and the concomitant growth of specialized media.[30]

George Steiner has put the case most cogently and eloquently. Modern man, he suggests, has come increasingly under pressure from the radical transformations of life brought on by the successive industrial, scientific, technological, and informational revolutions, and he has been acted upon by global, centrifugal forces that he can neither fully understand nor incorporate naturally into his daily existence. Seeking a stable psychic and social identity, man has responded by clinging to certain "atavisms of identity," by seeking roots against vertigo. This has produced an impulse to enclosure, thus making the "frontier" the dominant fact of international existence. In the collective sphere, the phenomenon is no less pronounced:

> The modern nation-state, the contemporary ideological cell, seeking to keep itself immune from challenge and from strangeness by means of hermetically sealed frontiers, is the enactment, on a collective scale, of the retreat of the individual into the burrow of his abandonment.[31]

This, then, brings us to the most immutable of the forces with which we must contend: ethnocentrism and its most virulent variant, nationalism. Ethnocentrism, of course, is an extraordinarily widespread phenomenon in all walks of life. Its characteristic features include: strong identification with one's own group and its culture, the tendency to see one's own group as the center of the universe, the tendency to perceive events in terms of one's own interests, the tendency to prefer one's own way of life (culture) over all others (seeing it as involving the best and right ways of acting, with an associated bias against other groups and their ways of acting), and a general suspicion of foreigners, their modes of thought, action, and motives.[32]

Nationalism derives from the continued adherence of virtually the entire human race to the independent nation-state as the preferred model of collective existence in the global arena. This has effectively precluded the emergence of enduring multinational enterprises—in the totalitarian world no less than in the free world. Even world order advocates, such as Robert Johansen, have expressed their frustration at this state of affairs:

Until an effective strategy is developed for implementing this vision [of world order], its very low political feasibility makes it unrealistic in the foreseeable future. Its implementation rests on agreement among national governments to restrict their sovereignty voluntarily. This is unlikely given present political attitudes and institutions.[33]

David Fromkin has argued persuasively that the independence of nations is the fundamental reality of our time. The fact of political fragmentation and the dream of political unity are the poles of discourse in the study of international relations. Such political fragmentation, Fromkin contends, is neither accidental nor arbitrary, but results instead from rooted patterns of behavior. What distinguishes states from individuals is that the latter have legal obligations to some higher authority. States, however, are unique in that they are completely independent. They are not ruled by anybody or anything else; there is no entity above them; they have no political superior; and there is no authority that they recognize and obey. At their worst, states are "beasts that roam the jungles of world politics, killing when they are hungry, and obeying no laws but those of their own nature."[34]

Fromkin goes on to suggest that we tend to overestimate the effect of alliances on the independence of states. Although it is usual to think that a permanent unity has been forged between allies that transcends the independent ambitions, rivalries, and desires of the particular states, in actuality an alliance is not a unity. It is, rather, an institutionalized diversity, in which the interests of the allies often are adverse to one another. Whatever unity of sentiment and action exists tends to be limited to the specific purposes for which the alliance was formed.[35]

Such circumstances have prompted Alistair Cooke to observe:

I do believe that since the invention of the intercontinental missile, patriotism has become the first refuge of unthinking men and women.

And it seems to me that among ourselves, among the nations of the Western Alliance, the leaders we have most to fear are those who talk about *national* destiny, who claim for their own people a nature superior to human nature.[36]

What is needed is what Robert Cooley Angell has termed "enlightened patriotism." Enlightened patriotism broadens traditional nationalism in two respects. First, the loyalty expressed is not that of an in-group, a nationality, but of the citizens of a territory. Second, it expresses a breadth of concern beyond the national territory itself— a concern which enlightenment about the interdependence of nations in the modern world produces. It is a sentiment halfway between traditional nationalism and loyalty to a world state.[37] If we are to appreciate the full import of Angell's vision, we first must understand the relationship that exists between alliance cohesion and consensus. It is through an understanding of this relationship that the crucial role of public opinion in determining the viability of the alliance will become clear.

COHESION, CONSENSUS, AND PUBLIC OPINION

Alliance cohesion, despite near-universal recognition of its importance to the sustained functioning of any alliance, is an elusive, little understood phenomenon. By common usage, it has come to embrace any and all of the following meanings:

- The ability of alliance partners to agree upon goals, strategy, and tactics, and to coordinate activities directed toward those goals.
- A synonym for alliance efficacy.
- The antonym of disintegration; that is, the ability of the coalition to survive.[38]

The factors most commonly mentioned as determinants of cohesion are: (1) the proximity and magnitude of the external threat; (2) the degree of ideological homogeneity within the alliance; and (3) the number of alliance members. Unfortunately, the precise effect these and other variables have on cohesion is ambiguous and therefore subject to diametrically opposed positions of seemingly equal validity. Other factors said to contribute to cohesion include: efficient communications between allies; a degree of economic interdependence; a larger range of common interests than expressed in the alliance; mutual confidence in the competence and military credibility and political dependability of allies; and a willingness to accept a division of labor on the alliance's military tasks. Conversely, among factors said to produce fragmentation and disintegration are: rigidity of organization; superpower domination; lack of consultation; domestic instability among partners; suspicion of allies; uncertainty as to the status of allies; uncertainties about the exact nature of the commitment; the presence of subgroups (or factions) within an alliance; the presence of different strategic priorities; differences in allied capabilities; ignorance about the decisionmaking structures of other allied governments; differences about issues not concerned with the alliance; and differences about the appropriate share of burdens, influence, and rewards.[39]

In the final analysis, such factors are not of metaphysical origin, but instead are manifestations of underlying congruencies or incongruencies in the value preferences of alliance members. Where there is widespread value congruency, consensus is approached and cohesion results. Consensus exists when—

> . . . the members of social systems are in a state of affirmative agreement about normative and cognitive matters relevant to their action towards one another, towards the central persons or roles in the system, and towards persons, roles, and collectivities outside the system. . . . Consensus connotes a solidarity formed by a sense of common identity arising from ties of personal affection, of primordial (ethnic, kinship, or territorial) characteristics, of a shared relationship to sacred things, of a membership in a common culture or in a common civil community.[40]

Ali Mazrui has identified four stages of interrelationship that may occur between diverse racial, national, and cultural groups in the world. The minimum degree of integration is a relationship of bare *coexistence* between distinct social identities. Such groups need not even know of each other's existence. They share a world but not a consciousness of that world's extent. The second degree of interrelationship is one of *contact,* which means that the different social groups have at least minimal dealings with each other or communication between each other. They need not be on friendly terms. The third degree of integration between social groups is a relationship of *compromise.* By this time, the dealings between the groups have become sufficiently complex, diverse, and interdependent to require a climate of peaceful reconciliation among the conflicting interests. The groups or nations still have clearly distinct identities, as well as distinct interests. But the process of national integration now has produced a capacity for the constant discovery of areas of compatibility. Between this stage of compromise and the fourth stage of *coalescence,* the process of convergence starts. From a cultural point of view, convergence is a process that either creates or discovers a growing sector of shared tastes, emotions, images, and values. Cultural convergence need not result in the total coalescence of previously distinct systems. Convergence may combine cultural diversity with cultural sharing. But when convergence goes beyond a certain point, the stage of coalescence is reached. Here consensus resides.[41]

True consensus is not majority opinion, nor is it a compromise solution. For that matter, neither is it an intellectual herding phenomenon. It is the condition that exists when the various parties to a controversial issue think as one on fundamental principles. It is the ability and the willingness to accept the legitimacy of opposing points of view without losing sight of a greater good that is being served. Even though disagreement on particulars should be expected—and even encouraged—there exists a sort of "spontaneous unanimity" on basics. The intellectual (and emotional) bonding that results is the overriding prerequisite for bona fide alliance cohesion.[42]

This conception of consensus represents an institutionalization of thought and action much like that embodied in German sociologist Arnold Gehlen's general theory of institutions.[43] Gehlen understands human institutions as substitutes for the reliable instincts that *homo sapiens* lacks as compared to other mammals. This means that institutions function to provide firm and reliable programs that individuals can follow at a low level of awareness—automatically, unthinkingly, "spontaneously." Every human society consists of a "background" of firmly programed activity and a "foreground" in which individuals can innovate. Institutionalization is the process by which items that were previously in the foreground—that is, were fully attended to and deliberately performed—are transposed into this background of automatized programs.

When an individual begins to reflect, deliberate, and weigh options in any given sphere of life, Gehlen suggests, it soon becomes impossible for the individual to act in the spontaneous, self-assured manner that every institutional program requires. What is peculiar to modern society is a very high degree of reflectiveness, deliberation, and choice—all features of rationalized consciousness. This aspect of modern consciousness is inimical to institutions, of whatever content, and it means that modern social order is peculiarly unstable, unreliable, and vulnerable to disintegration.

If consensus is the foundation on which cohesion is built, then most assuredly public opinion is the brick and mortar constituting that foundation. Where the institutionalization of thought and action has not taken root, where there is not a common framework of understanding, the "tyranny" of public opinion inevitably will rule the moment. There will, under such conditions, be no universally held truths, no unstated first principles that do not require constant revisitation. Reality will be enshrouded in a cloud of diffuse perceptions; every issue, however seemingly minor, will devolve into crisis; and collective action will stymie itself by self-induced entropy.

More than four decades ago, Harold Lasswell asserted that "democracy depends upon an alert and informed public opinion."[44] The force of these words assumes added meaning in the elevated pluralism of alliance decisionmaking, but largely for negative reasons. To begin with, there is no single, undifferentiated body of public opinion that acts upon—and can be acted upon by—government (this being, in Lasswell's view, the vital two-way connection that is the distinguishing mark of popular rule[45]). In the words of one authority;

> It is no longer adequate to use the panoplies of mass communication to address a hypothetical mass audience. There is no such thing; there are only congeries of group audiences. There are lots of specific publics, whose interests are quite various, and who only attend certain kinds of messages and certain communicators.[46]

Absent any measurable degree of consensus, the public opinion of an alliance is little more than a patchwork of attitudes and beliefs that reflects the diversity of audiences present. There are, first, distinctive national audiences defined by the sociocultural and linguistic peculiarities of their respective countries. Then there are, within each country, those characteristic groupings within the polity that are defined by their awareness of, and involvement in, public affairs—elite opinionmakers, the attentive public, and the mass (largely inattentive) public.[47] Finally, due to the effects of mass communications, there have emerged scores of "taste publics"—highly differentiated, specific groups whose value systems and identities are defined by the voluntary choices they have made in organizing their daily lives.[48] Because virtually any combination of demographic and life style characteristics may define these various taste publics, the challenge of identifying and accommodating their needs and desires represents a formidable task for policymakers.

In adjudging the relevance to alliance matters of Lasswell's ideas on public opinion and democracy, we also must not underestimate his emphasis on the *alert* and *informed* nature of such opinion. Little seems to have changed in this regard since Walter Lippmann opined in the 1920s that the democratic ideal of the omnicompetent, sovereign citizen is a false and unattainable ideal. The force of public opinion, he wrote, is partisan, spasmodic, simple-minded, and external (to the decisionmaking process)—not well-informed, continuously interested, nonpartisan, creative, and executive. We further must assume, said Lippmann, that the public is intermittent and inexpert in its curiousity; that it discerns only gross distinctions, is slow to be aroused, and quickly diverted; that, since it acts by aligning itself, it personalizes whatever it considers, and is interested only when events have been melodramatized as a conflict.[49]

This is a harsh indictment; yet it has the ring of truth to it. If, as some experts believe, the mass public makes up as much as 90 percent of the population, and its outlook on issues is conditioned less by accurate information and firm principles than by vague and fickle waves of emotionalism,[50] then the problem is bound to be magnified severalfold in the alliance context. The need for an institutional ethos therefore is self-evident. Unfortunately, NATO today does not come close to demonstrating those attributes commonly accepted as characteristic of a true institution:

- *External reality.* Even though NATO may be said to exist apart from its member states, it does not have a distinctive identity that would prompt one to say, for example, "I am from NATO," or "I am a NATO-ite."
- *Objectivity.* Not everyone agrees on precisely what NATO is, what "it" stands for, what "it" does, or what "its" objectives are.
- *Coercive power.* Like other supranational enterprises, NATO itself does not have organic means for exercising sanctions and exacting desired behaviors from member states. Its coercive power is all externally directed and, because that power is wielded by individual members, it is vulnerable to spontaneous impotence.
- *Moral authority.* NATO does not possess the inherent legitimacy necessary to command respect or allegiance from its members. The alliance may be said to command external respect from prospective adversaries, but only insofar as effective deterrence provides a useful measure of such tendencies.
- *Historicity.* NATO as a collective body does in fact have a history, although it is questionable whether it has developed a tradition (at least one worthy of emulation as a standard of excellence).[51]

Beyond this level of generality, there are a number of specific signs that NATO is a long way from achieving the unifying, lasting consensus so essential to the continued integrity of the alliance. If appropriate remedial action is to be taken, these signs require further elaboration.

NATO TODAY: A TRANSATLANTIC
PSYCHOLOGICAL GULF

Despite heated disagreement on how best to deal with the situation, few knowledgeable observers would deny the lack of cohesion that exists within the NATO alliance today. Among specialists on Atlantic affairs, the following comments are representative:

> Western Europe is a long way from the political consensus and institutional structures required to implement a European-wide security policy in the fullest sense of the term.[52]

> The stability of the Western alliance rests on a sense of shared values and interests between the United States and Western Europe; but that sense of mutual commitment may be deteriorating.[53]

> There is no Atlantic consensus, nor is there a European consensus.[54]

Statesmen, too—at least those no longer tied to formal diplomatic positions—are sensitive to this state of affairs. Henry Kissinger, for one, has argued that ". . . in nearly every [NATO] country the consensus on defense and foreign policy has broken down."[55] Such judgments are borne out by the results of various public opinion polls conducted over the past five years. These surveys suggest, among other things, that (a) neutralism in Europe is substantial and increasing; (b) many Europeans feel they are innocent bystanders caught between two superpowers; (c) distrust of American leadership is significant and growing; (d) Americans themselves are in no mood for an active international role, and they see themselves bearing an unfair share of the West's defense burden; (e) Western publics are far more concerned with domestic economic issues than with foreign policy and defense issues; and (f) there is no mandate in any Western country for substantially strengthening defense. Perhaps most importantly, many surveys show not only that American and European attitudes are widely different, but also that attitudes vary among European countries.[56]

With characteristic insight, Stanley Hoffmann has identified four major reasons for the current discord that divides alliance members: geography, history, domestic politics, and national character (or political culture). The last of these factors is especially noteworthy, for the issue of cultural divergence is seen by some as the single most important long-term contributor to a gradual drifting apart of the United States and Western Europe. Hoffmann cites three lines of cultural cleavage. The first concerns differing conceptions of simplicity versus complexity. Whereas Americans prefer simple policies (and explanations) to complex ones and tend to interpret Soviet behavior in particular in terms of a coherent, deliberate plan, West European leaders tend to have a more developed sense of the nuances of power politics and thus eschew overly simplistic solutions. A second line of cultural cleavage is the contrasting attitudes toward conflict that exist on the two sides of the Atlantic. Americans sometimes project on others the idea that force is a privileged tool on behalf of one's mission. West Europeans are generally more Clausewitzian in orientation and tend to be more concerned with the overall correlation of forces than with the balance (or imbalance) of military force. They look at international affairs less as a duel with swords, more as a game played with a whole range of cards. Finally, the United States is still (or again) in the throes of "exceptionalism"—the belief in the unique mission of America. This tends to promote a peculiar kind of insecurity: the need to ask oneself at every moment if one still is number one, if one is up to the task, faithful to the mandate. It also makes it difficult for Americans to understand experiences different from their own. The politics of Western Europe, by contrast, are not those of exceptionalism but those of survival. When the Cold War intensifies, dangers for survival and political autonomy increase, giving rise to the two tendencies of either wanting to opt out altogether or else of working to improve the atmosphere.[57]

The most disturbing aspect of this cultural divergence is that it represents such a pronounced departure from the past. During the early years of the Cold War and for a number of years thereafter, there was broad cultural sympathy between the United States and Europe. An especially powerful bond existed at the elite level between those who had run the war effort against Germany and Japan and who then assumed important peacetime roles on both sides of the Atlantic. The shared experiences of the war tended to reinforce a common cultural heritage that found its clearest expression in American elite education. Close European ties existed at the popular level as well. Vast immigration had established strong ethnic constituencies in America that remained intensely concerned with the fate of their homelands. By the same token, postwar Europe became closely attached to American scientific, technological, and economic developments, while also demonstrating a strong affinity for our popular culture.

Today the situation is markedly different. The simple passing of time and the dying out of the postwar "Atlanticist" elite have depleted the accumulated store of shared experiences and shared values. The United States, in attempting to come to grips with its own evolving racial and ethnic diversity, has been experiencing for some time now a "de-Europeanization," especially in its educational system. There continues to be a major shift in immigration into the United States, from European and Canadian sources to Latin American, Asian, and African sources. Increasingly, the new generations of Americans of European descent not only do not feel like Europeans living in America but display considerable ignorance of, and even hostility toward, their heritage. Similar tendencies are evident in Europe, where the United States seems less and less an ideal to be imitated.[58]

This so-called "successor generation" phenomenon has become an object of growing concern in many quarters, largely because of its portents for alliance cohesion. Born after World War II and free of the historical experiences and values that shaped their elders' views, the individuals constituting the successor generation are the educated elite most likely to assume roles of leadership and to set the agenda for their countries over the next two decades. Generally speaking, their values are "post-materialist" in nature—reflecting a preference for quality of life issues, self-realization, decentralized participation in decisionmaking, and a devaluation of the utility of military force in international politics. Although raised on high expectations of prosperity, reform, and detente, these individuals have been faced with worsening job markets and a deterioration of East-West relations. The resultant insecurity has fostered a growing disillusionment with technology, scientific progress, and "the system." This combination of post-materialist values and latent insecurity has been instrumental in feeding the antiestablishment, neonationalist, political activist urges so prevalent throughout Western Europe today. Most experts believe this to be a long-term, generational trend—not merely the transitory passions of youth.[59]

As we look to the future, we can expect to see an accentuation of two "divisive and unprecedented" trends. The first will be the emergence of a more-or-less permanent transatlantic psychological gulf brought on by the deep-seated mood shifts that are occurring among American and European elites and mass publics alike. The second will be an increasing intrusion of the mass public into foreign policy. As Western publics become more aware and active politically, and as they grow increasingly disenchanted with the competence of established political institutions and leaders, they will insert themselves ever more vigorously into the affairs of state. The confluence of these two trends may well have mutually reinforcing disruptive effects. On the one hand, as the public intervenes in alliance affairs, policymakers will have less and less latitude—even when they are willing to compromise—to settle transatlantic disputes by mutual give-and-take. On the other hand, mood shifts on both sides of the Atlantic—principally divergent in thrust—will work directly against any desire to compromise, much less to achieve consensus.[60]

Successful accommodation of these trends and the eventual establishment (or reestablishment) of a bona fide consensus within the alliance will depend, of course, on our ability to recognize and deal with two sets of factors addressed earlier: (1) our own ingrained attitudes toward "alliance democracy," and (2) those mediating forces in the contemporary international environment that tend to impede any efforts at multinational integration. At the same time, we must come to grips with two subtle influences that seem forever destined to impinge on our ability to forge an Atlantic consensus. The first of these is what Hugh Seton-Watson referred to as the "European mystique"—a common cultural heritage that exerts an imperceptible pull on all Europeans, East and West, and provides the inchoate stirrings of a transcendent allegiance that over time could lead to a real European community. Thus, calls for German reunification are but the most visible manifestations of historically bred cultural affinities that actually may produce stronger attractions between states on different sides of the Iron Curtain than between Western Europe and the United States.[61]

A countervailing influence that must be dealt with is the peculiarly American form of ethnocentrism that has been nurtured since this country's birth. The isolation of the United States for a century and a half after independence—the fact that we, unlike our European brethren, had no need to deal with powerful but culturally diverse neighbors—meant that America never developed a strong foreign policy tradition. European governments historically had no choice but to accept the fact that there were foreigners with whom they constantly had to interact, people who viewed matters differently and whose languages had to be learned merely to cope with them effectively. American culture, in contrast, has been more concerned with emancipating itself from foreign influence than with assimilating it. Our lack of significant experience as a colonial power, though salutary in other respects, had the residual negative effect of never forcing us to become sensitive to, and appreciative of, others. In a sense, we have taken perverse pride in being quite ignorant of the attitudes, traditions, and perceptions of foreign cultures. The growing bias of American education toward technology and away from the humanities seems almost certain to accentuate rather than ameliorate this self-imposed provincialism.[62] One result, almost assuredly, will be to hamper any efforts we might otherwise make to achieve some degree of unity (or at least harmony) with our NATO allies.

A NEW PUBLIC OPINION STRATEGY

For the major powers of the world, strategy in the modern era has become fundamentally an exercise in the management of perceptions. The arena of conflict is the human mind (and its emotional symbiont, the human heart), not a piece of terrain, a stretch of sea, or a sector of airspace. This conception of strategic interaction is frustratingly esoteric and alien to most Americans, who continue to adhere to a paradigm of warfare in which military force is the actualization, rather than the symbolic instrumentality, of strategy. Consequently, we find ourselves prisoners of a mindset totally ill-equipped to deal with the threat facing us in Europe today.

U.S. strategy in Europe must be designed to provide a direct counter to Soviet strategy. If the Soviets in fact seek to fragment NATO by exploiting the psychological vulnerabilities of the alliance, then we must seek just as assiduously to turn those vulnerabilities into strengths, to reverse the emerging trend of alienation and polarization, to create one mind where now there are many. Our objective must be to forge a new consensus within the alliance. We can achieve this objective only if we are willing to accord public opinion a central role in our strategic thinking and planning.

Grethe Vaerno, a member of the Norwegian Parliament, has called for the formulation of a NATO public opinion strategy as a necessary precursor to the reestablishment of consensus and support for Western security policy. The alliance must decide in concert, she argues, on a strategy that can stand up to public scrutiny and win broad public support. Accordingly, the need for a public opinion strategy is every bit as urgent as the need for a military strategy.[63]

Considering the growing influence of the general public in the international affairs of democratic societies, traditional government-to-government diplomacy has shown itself to be no longer a fully adequate tool of modern statecraft. Traditionalists, of course, take umbrage at the suggestion that the essence of power politics is the manipulation of symbols to create desired images in the minds of target audiences. Yet, it is precisely because of the importance of the perceptual dimension that an effective public opinion strategy must be built primarily around the major elements of *public* diplomacy available to national decisionmakers: propaganda, information, and cultural exchange. Collectively, these instruments of power provide the necessary means to ensure that (a) other nations more accurately understand this country, its values, institutions, and policies; (b) our understanding of other nations and of our interrelationship with them is informed and accurate;

(c) this mutual understanding is bolstered by collaborative individual and institutional relationships across cultural lines; and (d) as the international policies of our government are formed, we take into account the values, interests, and priorities of publics abroad.[64]

The public opinion strategy envisioned here would embody five major elements. The first of these elements would be to focus principally on NATO audiences rather than on the Soviet Union and its Warsaw Pact subjects. Although public diplomacy clearly has experienced a new awakening under the Reagan Administration, the preponderant emphasis seemingly has been on propaganda targeted at Soviet and East European audiences. Such an approach suffers from two inherent shortcomings. First, it ignores decades of communications research which suggests, among other things, that (a) individuals generally hear only what they want to hear and thus tend to be most responsive to messages that reinforce established predispositions; and (b) ideological—especially counterideological—themes tend not to stimulate other than superficial acknowledgment by recipients. Second, it is quite likely that U.S. propaganda targeted at the Eastern bloc simply heightens the innate insecurity and xenophobia of the Soviets by adding to the conviction that they are constantly under siege by foreign enemies.[65]

Marshall Shulman has lent the reasoned judgment of his expertise to this issue by noting:

> Our capacity to influence the nature of change in the Soviet Union is limited. . . . The main objective of our policy should . . . be to respond to the Soviet challenge in ways that will protect our security, our interests, and our values, rather than to try to force changes in the Soviet Union or to bring about changes in its foreign policy indirectly by seeking to undermine the Soviet system.[66]

We stand to gain most by concentrating our efforts on allied audiences, with whom we have an established, even if unstable, foundation of cultural and philosophical compatibility. This will entail a commitment on our part to understand better the complex array of psychological attachments within the alliance today that we have deluded ourselves into thinking we already understand. It also will entail the actuation of specific measures to awaken and nurture "natural" but dormant inclinations toward common Euro-American values.

The second major element of this strategy would be to focus on the various audiences constituting the mass public rather than on elite opinionmakers or the attentive public. The traditional emphasis of both private and public diplomacy has been on the latter two groups—the underlying presumption being that only those who actively engage in national security affairs, either as leaders or as committed followers, are worthy of attention. The weakness of this increasingly outmoded logic lies not merely in the fact that the mass public has begun to assert itself more vigorously on defense and foreign policy matters, but also in the fact that the informed segments of any population typically are the most committed to particular points of view. Their sophistication on the sometimes-arcane aspects of national security makes them also the most difficult audience(s) to penetrate and convince.

The mass public, in contrast, because it tends to be passive and inert, is much more malleable and subject to manipulation—provided that its specific interests and values can be diagnosed and exploited as "triggers" to some other desired response. Furthermore, the more aware and democratic a society becomes, the less deference is apt to be shown to so-called experts. Consequently, the success of elites depends increasingly on their ability to mobilize mass support. This has prompted one authority to observe:

> The critical group in molding a consensus is the large segment of the society that is not strongly supportive of social change but is 'able to live' with it. If one threatens them or frightens them too much and applies too much pressure to them, their willingness to live with social change will be converted into reactionary panic.[67]

The third, and clearly the most central, element of this strategy calls for the coordinated employment of all the instruments of public diplomacy at our disposal—but with a pronounced emphasis on cultural exchange first, information programs second, and propaganda third. These priorities commonly tend to be reversed—propaganda being considered the only means of achieving immediate impact, and cultural exchange capable of producing only long-term, difficult-to-measure results. In point of fact, though, cultural exchange offers the most subtle, unobtrusive, and lasting means of influencing friendly or neutral opinions abroad. But, whereas cultural exchange traditionally has been aimed primarily at elite audiences—academicians and parliamentarians, for example, whose views already are well-developed and firmly held—the intent here would be to reach down into the mass publics of the various NATO countries (including our own) and attempt to build influence at the grass roots level. We would be practicing, in essence, a sort of "co-optation by flattery" by selecting members of that segment of the population most often ignored by foreign policy establishments, funding their travel elsewhere within the alliance, and seeking to build empathy and understanding through exposure to citizens and policymakers from allied countries. Ideally, this would have the effect of creating psychological "fifth columns" capable of being a force in their own right—increasingly invulnerable to manipulation by aggressive single-interest groups and more appreciative of the inherent complexities of international affairs with which decisionmakers must contend.

For the information and propaganda dimensions of the strategy to work most effectively, they must be integrated almost to the point of complete convergence—propaganda becoming more like information, and information more like propaganda. This will require the adoption of a much more sophisticated understanding of propaganda than presently exists in this country. Most Americans suffer from a phobia of propaganda, viewing it basically as a "black art" employed for evil purposes. Furthermore, we continue to embrace the rather simplistic notion that there is truth, then there is propaganda.[68] Unfortunately, as we must come to realize, in the realm of international politics there is no metaphysical truth; there is only *our* truth and *their* truth. The objective is to convince as many audiences as possible that our truth is the preferred point of view. Propaganda in this sense becomes a form of civic eduation—the design being in the present context to stimulate a new consciousness among the various peoples of the Atlantic Alliance that they are citizens of NATO. Thus, there is little to distinguish between propaganda and education.

> The standard of education is the truth of the material in the light of available knowledge. The standard of propaganda is the purpose behind the teaching. Where the purpose is achieved by the teaching of what is believed to be the truth then the result is both propaganda and education.[69]

Our use of propaganda must reflect a concern with both substance and style—the underlying premise being that increasingly aware publics are both sensitive and averse to even the hint of manipulation. If we are to avoid the appearance of thought control, our message must be subtle in manner and tone—neither hortatory and polemical nor sanctimonious and condescending. Our message also must give every evidence of being factual and objective rather than value-laden (even though the transmission of values is what we hope to achieve). Moreover, it must appear, wherever possible, to emanate from respectable independent sources (e.g., foundations, international research institutions, etc.), so as to dilute the perception of governmental intrusion.

The fourth element of this strategy would be to place added emphasis on reestablishing confidence among the NATO peoples in the leadership of the alliance. Grethe Vaerno has pointed out that the leadership crisis within NATO is perhaps the most serious obstacle to a consensus on the vital and complicated issues facing us today. The mood is one of complete distrust. Because leaders repeatedly have been proven wrong, there is a sense now that everyone's opinion is equal to everyone else's.[70]

We might be well-advised in this regard to recall the views of Walter Lippmann, who theorized that what the public does is not to express its opinions directly, but to align itself for or against a proposal. Thus, contrary to the popular conception of democracy, the people do not actually govern by expressing their will; instead, they periodically mobilize to support or oppose the individuals who do govern. It is the power to discern who these individuals are that Lippman believed is the ultimate objective of educating public opinion.[71]

The fifth and final element of this strategy is based on the realization that consensus is a cumulative phenomenon. Its existence at one level depends in no small measure on whether it exists at lower levels. Alliance consensus, in other words, is far more likely to obtain where there is consensus within the individual member nations of the pact. The question that must be answered is whether the latter is an absolute precondition for the former.

In speaking of the steady erosion of national unity that has occurred in Great Britain since 1945, Michael Howard has observed that the abandonment of the nation as a focus for loyalty means that loyalties focus not at a higher level, but at a lower level: upon class, or region, or sect, or race, or simply upon gangs. He argues, therefore, that while it is eminently desirable to move from lower to higher loyalties—from Britain to Europe or to Commonwealth or the Atlantic Community; ultimately to the Planet Earth—this can be done effectively only if the roots of national loyalty are first well-nourished.[72]

Howard's argument is intuitively compelling, for it speaks to the only experience we have ever known. Who among us, never having given fealty to anything beyond the nation-state, can imagine committing ourselves to such an unknown ideal? We must ask ourselves, though, whether the fragmentation at the national level, of which Howard speaks, is not indicative of a larger evolutionary trend that we seek foolishly to resist. It may well be that the reason there is a tendency to revert to lower-level loyalties is because there never has been a suitable higher-level alternative. This we must seek to provide. Thus, even as we seek consensus at the national level, so too must we proceed apace to achieve consensus at the alliance level, for it is the latter that promises ultimately to determine how successful our passage into the future will be.

NOTES

1. Alan Ned Sabrosky, "Allies, Clients, and Encumbrances," *International Security Review* (Summer 1980), pp. 117–149.

2. See, for example, Michael Smith, *Western Europe and the United States: The Uncertain Alliance* (London: George Allen & Unwin, 1984); Stanley Hoffmann, "The Western Alliance: Drift or Harmony?" *International Security* (Fall 1981), pp. 105–125; Robert E. Hunter, "Rift and Drift in the Atlantic Alliance," *Washington Quarterly* (Summer 1984), pp. 126–132; Eliot A. Cohen, "The Long-Term Crisis of the Alliance," *Foreign Affairs* (Winter 1982/83), pp. 325–343; and *The Trans-Atlantic Crisis: A Conference of the Committee for the Free World* (New York: The Orwell Press, 1982). Also see Theodore Draper, "The Western Misalliance," *Washington Quarterly* (Winter 1981), pp. 13–68; and Edward A. Kolodziej, "Europe: The Partial Partner," *International Security* (Winter 1980/81), pp. 104–131.

3. Richard J. Barnet, "The Atlantic Alliance," *Bulletin of the Atomic Scientists* (January 1984), pp. 8–10; Irving Kristol, "NATO Needs Shock Treatment," *Reader's Digest* (February 1984), pp. 165–168.

4. Earl C. Ravenal, "Europe Without America: The Erosion of NATO," *Foreign Affairs* (Summer 1985), pp. 1020–1035. For a similar view, see Laurence Radway, "U.S. Forces in Europe: The Case for Cautious Contraction," *SAIS Review* (Winter-Spring 1985), pp. 227–242.

5. *Ibid.*

6. For perhaps the most thorough recent assessment of the state of research on alliance dynamics, see Michael Don Ward, *Research Gaps in Alliance Dynamics* (Denver, CO: Graduate School of International Studies, University of Denver, 1984), esp. pp. 27–39, which deals with various aspects of cohesion.

7. George H. Quester, "The Future of the American NATO Commitment," in William A. Buckingham, Jr. (ed.), *Defense Planning for the 1990s* (Washington, DC: National Defense University Press, 1984), pp. 109–137.

8. Michael Howard, "Reassurance and Deterrence: Western Defence in the 1980s," *Foreign Affairs* (Winter 1982/83), pp. 309–324.

9. Josef Joffe, "Europe's American Pacifier," *Foreign Policy* (Spring 1984), pp. 64–82.

10. Robert W. Tucker, "The Atlantic Alliance and Its Critics," *Commentary* (May 1982), pp. 63–72.

11. Sun Tzu, *The Art of War,* trans. by Samuel B. Griffith (London: Oxford University Press, 1963), pp. 77–78.

12. David M. Abshire, "NATO at the Moral Crossroads," *Washington Quarterly* (Summer 1984), pp. 3–12.

13. Edward N. Luttwak, *The Grand Strategy of the Soviet Union* (New York: St. Martin's Press, 1983), pp. 86–88.

14. For example, see Robert J. Art, "Fixing Atlantic Bridges," *Foreign Policy* (Spring 1982), pp. 67–85; Alun Chalfont, "The Great Unilateralist Illusion," *Encounter* (April 1983), pp. 18–38, and "Stormy Atlantic Weather," *Encounter* (January 1983), pp. 9–16; and Kenneth Rush, "NATO: 35 Years of Deterrence," *American Legion Magazine* (January 1985), pp. 20, 21, 44, 46.

15. Coit Dennis Blacker, "The Soviet Perception of European Security," in Derek Leebaert (ed.), *European Security: Prospects for the 1980s* (Lexington, MA: Lexington Books, 1979), pp. 137–161.

16. Richard Nixon, *The Real War* (New York: Warner Books, 1980), esp. Chapter 2 (pp. 17–45).

17. For a full treatment of these ideas, see John Lenczowski, *Soviet Perceptions of U.S. Foreign Policy* (Ithaca, NY: Cornell University Press, 1982), pp. 27–60. Also, see Edwina Moreton and Gerald Segal (eds.), *Soviet Strategy Toward Western Europe* (London: George Allen & Unwin, 1984), esp. Karen Dawisha's chapter, "Soviet Ideology and Western Europe," pp. 19–38.

18. An excellent disquisition on the influence of Sun Tzu in Soviet strategy is to be found in Tomas Ries, "Sun Tzu and Soviet Strategy," *International Defense Review* (4/1984), pp. 389–392.

19. Lenczowski, *op. cit.*

20. Richard H. Shultz and Roy Godson, *Dezinformatsia: Active Measures in Soviet Strategy* (Washington, DC: Pergamon-Brassey's, 1984), pp. 2, 40.

21. Lawrence S. Eagleburger, "Unacceptable Intervention: Soviet Active Measures," *Officer Review* (November 1983), pp. 1–3.

22. Elizabeth Teague, "The Kremlin & the Peace Fighters," *Encounter* (July/August 1985), pp. 73–77. Also, see Vladimir Bukovsky, "The Peace Movement & the Soviet Union," *Commentary* (May 1982), pp. 25–41.

23. Robert A. Dahl, *Dilemmas of Pluralist Democracy: Autonomy vs. Control* (New Haven, CT: Yale University Press, 1982), p. 6.

24. *Ibid.*, p. 7.

25. Robert A. Dahl, *A Preface to Democratic Theory* (Chicago, IL: University of Chicago Press, 1956), p. 35.

26. *Ibid.*, p. 124.

27. For fuller discussion of the Wilsonian paradigm, see Vincent Ostrom, *The Intellectual Crisis in American Public Administration* (University, AL: University of Alabama Press, 1974), pp. 26–29. Also see Gregory D. Foster, "Wilsonian Political Thought and the Prospects for World Government in the Century Ahead," in Jack Rabin and James S. Bowman (eds.), *Politics and Administration: Woodrow Wilson and American Public Administration* (New York: Marcel Dekker, Inc., 1984), pp. 277–295.

28. For example, see James R. Huntley, "The Alliance of Democracies: A New Strategy," *Washington Quarterly* (Autumn 1983), pp. 53–61; and Ray S. Cline, "A New Grand Strategy for the United States: An Essay," *Comparative Strategy* (Vol. 1, Nos. 1/2, 1978), pp. 1–11. Also see the arguments of Jean-Francois Revel, "Can the Democracies Survive?" *Commentary* (June 1984), pp. 19–28, and the letters to the editor prompted by that article in *Commentary* (October 1984), pp. 18–23.

29. Walenty Nowacki, *Civilization and Logic: The Law of Inversely Proportional Stupidity* (Forest Hills, NY: NOW Mail Order Books, 1983).

30. James E. Gruning, "Turning McLuhan on His Head," in Gruning (ed.), *Decline of the Global Village* (Bayside, NY: General Hall, Inc., 1976), pp. 3–20.

31. George Steiner, "Borders and the Modern Mind," *Harper's* (August 1984), pp. 13–14.

32. Ken Booth, *Strategy and Ethnocentrism* (New York: Holmes & Meier, 1979), p. 15.

33. Robert C. Johansen, *The National Interest and the Public Interest* (Princeton, NJ: Princeton University Press, 1980), p. 31.

34. David Fromkin, *The Independence of Nations* (New York: Praeger, 1981), pp. xiii, xiv, 15–17, 19, 121.

35. *Ibid.,* pp. 114–119.

36. Alistair Cooke, "The United States and Europe: A Wary Friendship," *Parameters* (Summer 1984), pp. 3–9.

37. Robert Cooley Angell, *The Quest for World Order* (Ann Arbor: University of Michigan Press, 1979), pp. 52–54.

38. Ole R. Holsti, P. Terrence Hopmann, and John D. Sullivan, *Unity and Disintegration in International Alliances: Comparative Studies* (New York: John Wiley & Sons, 1973), p. 16.

39. Ken Booth, "Alliances," in John Baylis, Ken Booth, John Garnett, and Phil Williams, *Contemporary Strategy: Theories and Policies* (New York: Holmes & Meier, 1975), pp. 172–191. Also see Arlene Idol Broadhurst, "Speculation on Abstract Perspectives: NATO and the Warsaw Pact," in Broadhurst (ed.), *The Future of European Alliance Systems: NATO and the Warsaw Pact* (Boulder, CO: Westview, 1982), pp. 39–67.

40. G. Duncan Mitchell, ed., *A Dictionary of Sociology* (London: Routledge and Kegan Paul, 1968), pp. 40–43.

41. Ali A. Mazrui, "World Culture and the Search for Human Consensus," in Saul H. Mendlovitz (ed.), *On the Creation of a Just World Order* (New York: The Free Press, 1975), pp. 1–37.

42. Fuller discussion of the author's views on consensus is contained in Gregory D. Foster, "Consensus and National Security Policy," *The Bureaucrat* (Fall 1982), pp. 49–53. Herbert McClosky, "Consensus and Ideology in American Politics," *The American Political Science Review* (June 1964), pp. 361–379 has suggested as a practical measure of consensus that there be a level of agreement of 75 percent or more on a given question. This figure, though arbitrary, is realistically modest (falling as it does midway between a bare majority and unanimity), and it has been designated in this country and elsewhere as the extraordinary majority required for certain constitutional purposes.

43. Gehlen's theory of institutions frequently is referenced in the writings of American sociologist Peter Berger. For example, see Peter L. Berger and Hansfried Kellner, *Sociology Reinterpreted* (Garden City, NY: Anchor Books, 1981), pp. 155–157.

44. Harold D. Lasswell, *Democracy Through Public Opinion* (George Banta Publishing Company, 1941), p. 16.

45. *Ibid.,* p. 15.

46. H. L. Nieburg, *Public Opinion: Tracking and Targeting* (New York: Praeger, 1984), p. 29.

47. This three-tiered typology is developed in James N. Rosenau, *Public Opinion and Foreign Policy* (New York: Random House, 1961), pp. 27–41. A

more detailed, five-tiered typology is suggested in Gabriel Almond, "Public Opinion and National Security Policy," *Public Opinion Quarterly* (Vol. 20, 1956), pp. 371–378.

48. Nieburg, *op. cit.*, p. 33.

49. Walter Lippmann, *The Phantom Public* (New York: Harcourt, Brace and Company, 1925), pp. 39, 64–65, 151. Also see Lippman's earlier book on the subject, *Public Opinion* (New York: The Free Press, 1922).

50. This estimate of the size of the mass public is offered by Mark N. Hagopian, *Regimes, Movements, and Ideologies* (New York: Longman, 1978), pp. 371–372. A much more conservative estimate—30 percent of the population—is suggested in Bruce Russett and Harvey Starr, *World Politics: The Menu for Choice* (San Francisco, CA: W. H. Freeman and Company, 1981), p. 242.

51. This list of institutional characteristics is defined by Peter L. Berger and Brigitte Berger, *Sociology: A Biographical Approach* (New York: Basic Books, 1972), pp. 72–83.

52. Stanley R. Sloan, "European Co-operation and the Future of NATO," *Survival* (November/December 1984), pp. 242–251.

53. William Schneider, "Elite and Public Opinion: The Alliance's New Fissure?" *Public Opinion* (February/March 1983), pp. 5–8, 51.

54. Humphrey Taylor, "Nine Nations Assess Economic and Security Issues," *Public Opinion* (August/September 1983), pp. 16–17, 54–55.

55. Henry A. Kissinger, "Issues Before the Atlantic Alliance," *Washington Quarterly* (Summer 1984), pp. 132–144.

56. Taylor, "Nine Nations."

57. Hoffmann, "The Western Alliance." Also see Kim R. Holmes, "Europeanizing NATO," *Washington Quarterly* (Spring 1984), pp. 59–68. Holmes points out the tendency of European intellectuals to portray Europe as a land of cultural sophistication and community ideals, in contrast to the banal and libertarian popular culture of the United States. For a cynical critique of this European tendency, see Owen Harries, "European 'Sophistication' vs. American 'Naivete'," *Commentary* (December 1983), pp. 46–50.

58. For discussion of these general themes, see David P. Calleo, "The Atlantic Alliance: A View From America," in Frans A. M. Alting von Geusau (ed.), *Allies in a Turbulent World* (Lexington, MA: Lexington Books, 1982), pp. 3–19; Michael Smith, *Western Europe and the United States*, pp. 48–49; and Robert R. Bowie, "The Bases for Postwar Cooperation," in Karl Kaiser and Hans-Peter Schwarz (eds.), *America and Western Europe: Problems and Prospects* (Lexington, MA: Lexington Books, 1977), pp. 47–62. Current immigration trends are discussed in Nathan Glazer, "Ethnicity—North, South, West," *Commentary* (May 1982), pp. 73–78.

59. See Stephen F. Szabo, "Brandt's Children: The West German Successor Generation," *Washington Quarterly* (Winter 1984), pp. 50–59; Szabo (ed.), *The Successor Generation: International Perspectives of Postwar Europeans* (London: Butterworths, 1983); and Helena Page, "Reunification and the Successor Generation in Germany," *Washington Quarterly* (Winter 1984), pp. 60–68.

60. An exceptionally well-done expansion on these ideas is presented in Michael R. Gordon, "Mood Contrasts and NATO," *Washington Quarterly* (Winter 1985), pp. 107–130.

61. See Hugh Seton-Watson, "What is Europe, Where is Europe?" *Encounter* (July/August 1985), pp. 9–17.

62. For further development of these ideas, see Michael Howard, "The Bewildered American Raj," *Harper's* (March 1985), pp. 55–60.

63. Grethe Vaerno, "A Public Opinion Strategy," *NATO Review* (Vol. 31, No. 3/4, 1983), pp. 26–31.

64. These fundamental purposes of public diplomacy were articulated by former Deputy Secretary of State Warren Christopher. Quoted in Allen C. Hansen, *USIA: Public Diplomacy in the Computer Age* (New York: Praeger, 1984), p. 3.

65. For useful discussions of public diplomacy, see David I. Hitchcock, Jr., "Publics & Policy," *Foreign Service Journal* (April 1985), pp. 26–29; Carnes Lord, "In Defense of Public Diplomacy," *Commentary* (April 1984), pp. 42–50; John Spicer Nichols, "Wasting the Propaganda Dollar," *Foreign Policy* (Fall 1984), pp. 129–140; and John M. Oseth, "Repairing the Balance of Images: U.S. Public Diplomacy for the Future," *Naval War College Review* (July-August 1985), pp. 52–66.

66. Marshall D. Shulman, "What the Russians Really Want: A Rational Response to the Soviet Challenge," *Harper's* (April 1984), pp. 63–71.

67. Andrew M. Greeley, *Building Coalitions* (New York: Franklin Watts, 1974), p. 119.

68. Perhaps the clearest expression of this notion in the postwar era was President Harry Truman's April 20, 1950 speech to the American Society of Newspaper Editors, in which he observed that one of the greatest tasks facing the free nations today is "to meet false propaganda with truth all around the globe. Everywhere we must meet it and overcome it with honest information about freedom and democracy." See Harry S. Truman, "Fight False Propaganda With Truth," *Vital Speeches of the Day* (May 1, 1950), pp. 442–444.

69. Terrence H. Qualter, *Propaganda and Psychological Warfare* (New York: Random House, 1962), p. 21.

70. Vaerno, "A Public Opinion Strategy."

71. Lippmann, *The Phantom Public,* pp. 63–68.

72. Michael Howard, "Is Winston Churchill Still Relevant?" *Encounter* (April 1985), pp. 20–26.

6

CHANGING PATTERNS OF COLLECTIVE DEFENSE: U.S. SECURITY COMMITMENTS IN THE THIRD WORLD

Terry L. Deibel[1]

Most of the classic literature and much of the learned American commentary on U.S. alliances focuses on formal, treaty-based commitments in general, and on NATO in particular. Indeed, many scholars and government officials routinely refer to NATO simply as "*the* Alliance." Such habitual patterns of thought are not at all surprising, for the North Atlantic Treaty of 1949 was the first effective American military alliance in a century and a half and remains America's most important and elaborate defense tie. Moreover, virtually all of the alliances concluded during the decade after NATO's birth were embodied in formal treaties approved by the Senate.

Today, however, a focus limited to treaty-based relationships with the industrialized world would miss the most interesting and potentially significant developments in the American commitment posture overseas. From Morocco to the Philippines, and from Pakistan to Honduras, the United States is today as active as at any time in its history in recruiting new security partners and reinforcing old ones. More important, it is doing so under a rather different set of policy imperatives than in the past and in the face of fundamental changes in objective conditions to the South. These differing circumstances have made the commitment process a particularly difficult one, fraught with disappointment and sometimes dramatic reversals.

Indeed, the much-discussed crises in NATO—arising out of nuclear parity and declining U.S. credibility—are dwarfed in their scope and impact by the changes which complicate U.S.–Third World ties. Never

107

easy for Americans to understand and deal with, the Third World today suffers from accumulated debt and economic mismanagement, extremist religious fundamentalism, and growing demands for political participation, all of which accentuate its chronic instability. Into these tumultuous circumstances sails a Soviet policy emboldened by power projection capabilities of which Gorbachev's predecessors could only dream. Seeking to counter them, the United States faces a progressive loss of American-owned or controlled military facilities around the world, condemned despite the Reagan restoration to a generally weaker relative power position in a time of ever-expanding interests.

And yet, in spite or perhaps because of these difficulties, we are in the midst of the most intense American security interaction with the Third World ever. For the better part of a decade, and under the improbable combined leadership of Presidents Carter and Reagan, the U.S. Government has been creating a major new network of security commitments to the South, one different than any of the postwar period. But precisely because of the nature of these commitments, the process has been little noticed or analyzed. The time is long overdue to take stock, ask important questions, and project what the future may hold.

EARLY POSTWAR COMMITMENTS

The security relationships formed since 1979 are really the third set constructed by the United States since the country abandoned its historic aversion to alliances after World War II, and the three groups of U.S. alliances have differed quite dramatically in the motivation of American policymakers, the kinds of nations involved, and the shape of the resulting relationships. Appreciating the differences between them goes a long way towards understanding the current round of commitment creation.

The first set of American postwar security commitments was formed by President Harry S. Truman and his Secretary of State, Dean Acheson. These formal alliances were strategic in the broadest sense of the term; that is, they confirmed major changes in U.S. foreign policy as it turned from a hoped-for postwar condominium with the Soviet Union to face the realities of Cold War and the necessity of containment. In line with those changes, these commitments were designed to protect centers of industrial capacity that, though devastated by the recent war, were essential in the long run to the global balance of power: namely, Western Europe (including Britain), Japan, Australia, and New Zealand. As a result, they provided a real aggregation of power for deterrence and (if necessary) defense, although they were originally designed more as political, confidence-building measures for nations threatened by communist subversion than as military protection against outright attack.

Not incidentally, these alliances connected the United States to like-minded, advanced societies with which—in spite of our having just fought two of them in the world war—we shared a clear and deep complementarity of interests; indeed, the genius of that generation of postwar statesmen was largely in sensing the reality of those shared interests so soon after the war's end. And many of these relationships were underpinned by close personal and cultural ties, the result of historic immigration patterns, common language, or wartime cooperation. It is not surprising, then, that they are still our strongest security relationships—in spite of ANZUS disputes on nuclear ship visits, trade battles with Japan and Europe, or periodic NATO crises over out-of-area issues.

The second set of postwar American alliances, negotiated by Secretary of State John Foster Dulles during the Eisenhower administration, seems at first glance much like the Truman/Acheson undertakings. Most were based on formal treaties, consented to by the Senate and ratified by the president; in addition, they were often multilateral in character and included an organizational component. Thus, NATO and the ANZUS were joined by SEATO and (less directly) CENTO, the Mutual Security Treaty with Japan by pacts with South Korea and the Republic of China.

But beneath these superficial similarities lay an almost entirely different motive and character. Lacking the strategic purpose of Acheson's commitments, Dulles' alliances were tactical artifacts designed to make the Eisenhower strategy of massive retaliation credible in local situations. Just as today many Europeans find it hard to believe that Washington would risk New York by a strategic nuclear response to a Soviet conventional attack on West Germany, so in the 1950s many South Koreans, Taiwanese, Thai or Pakistanis found it difficult to credit an American atomic strike on Moscow in response to an ethnic insurgency, a border incident, or a neighbor's alliance with communism. When such inevitable crises in regional security occurred, Dulles' alliances filled the credibility gap. SEATO was signed to shore up Western positions in Indochina after Dien Bien Phu, CENTO was formed out of the Baghdad Pact when Moscow penetrated the Middle East via Nasser's Egypt, the alliance with Taiwan was designed to fend off China after its attacks on Quemoy and Matsu, and the treaty with South Korea was intended to stabilize the shaky armistice ending the Korean War.

Ad hoc responses thus used in emergencies to plug holes in the dikes of containment, the Eisenhower/Dulles alliances showed for the first time many of the disadvantages common to U.S. security commitments in the Third World. Although the countries embraced by these alliances may have had some importance to the balance of power as front-line states on the Dulles containment perimeter, they possessed little industrial capability and were hardly themselves critical weights in the scales of world power. Far too weak to help aggregate power, they instead required a good deal of American support; in fact, the Dulles pacts seemed to make the United States at least partially responsible for the existence of a number of authoritarian regimes. Of course, these states did provide power projection facilities to American forces and thus could be seen, given the military technology of the 1950s, as important to the protection of areas which were vital in themselves, either directly (like Korea to the defense of Japan) or indirectly (such as Middle East oil for the independence of Europe). But few cultural ties and little complementarity of interest underlay these commitments, and 25 years later all but the Korean treaty were gone.

They did not, of course, go quietly. It was in ostensible fulfillment of one of them, the SEATO treaty, that the United States fought in Vietnam, in the process destroying the domestic consensus on the containment policy itself. But it would be a mistake to look back on these alliances as foreign policy relics of a misguided era. For all their tactical improvisation, the idea of perimeter containment (and the Dulles alliances which supported it) was far more appropriate to an era of limited Soviet power-projection capabilities than to the military circumstances of our own day. Although these commitments absorbed American resources, they were easily affordable in a time when domestic social programs were only 6 percent of GNP and the American economy produced over 40 percent of the world's goods and services. Most important, they may well have provided the reassurance necessary to nurture the now-vibrant economies of the Pacific littoral, as well as the societal interconnections which are slowly building a sense of mutual interest and even cultural understanding. In ways he scarcely understood, Dulles may have built better then he knew.

THE NEW FACE OF U.S. SECURITY COMMITMENTS

The security commitments begun by President Carter in 1979 and expanded by the Reagan administration since 1981 are thus the third set to be negotiated since the end of World War II. Although these relationships share their Third World connection with the Dulles alliances, they are at least as different from both the Acheson and Dulles commitments as those two groups were from each other. Perhaps the major difference is that they have been much less directly embraced as explicit and first-order instruments of policy; instead, though hardly unintended, these commitments have been used to support other defense or foreign policy concerns or even arisen as the consequences of policy, taking nontreaty forms appropriate to that secondary or tertiary status. Although they are in one sense products of a resurgent America, the Carter/Reagan commitments reflect as well the massive changes in American power and policy which have characterized the post-Vietnam era.

Indeed, it is highly improbable that either Jimmy Carter or the voters who elected him in 1976 expected his administration to begin the reextension of American security commitments. After all, the decade before had seen the Tet offensive and the fall of Saigon, the eclipse of the U.S. relationship with Taiwan as part of the normalization of American relations with China, the passage in Congress of the War Powers Act and the Clark amendment prohibiting U.S. involvement in the Angolan civil war, the expulsion of the United States from its bases in Libya and Thailand, and the Nixon Doctrine, redefining many existing U.S. commitments to exclude the use of American combat forces. Carter campaigned on a 5 percent cut in the defense budget, and once in office he announced a plan to pull U.S. combat forces from South Korea, acquiesced in the demise of SEATO, twice failed to respond directly to invasions of Zaire, and offended Third World allies from Korea to Pakistan with his human rights and nuclear nonproliferation initiatives.

But this first Carter policy disappeared in the course of 1979, and with it ended the decade-long reduction of American security commitments in the Third World. Events that year seemed to show that the process of disengagement had gone too far, that vital American interests were being endangered by sinister forces that needed to be resisted. Renewed Vietnamese aggression in Indochina, the fundamentalist revolution and fall of the Shah in Iran, the second oil crisis and the return of gas lines in the United States, the triumph of the Sandinistas in Nicaragua, the onset of the Iranian hostage crisis, and the Soviet invasion of Afghanistan—all seemed to demand a radically different American response. Opinion polls registered a new popular recognition that some overseas American interests might be important enough to defend—even by military action—as well as a willingness to support the increased defense spending necessary for that task. Suddenly, the Carter administration froze its commitment reductions, then gradually began to strengthen old security ties and forge new ones.

In the Far East it postponed, then cancelled the Korean troop withdrawal plan; and in the summer of 1979 the President visited Seoul to proclaim that the American "military commitment to Korea's security is unshakable, strong and enduring."[2] Reversing the administration's ambiguous stance after SEATO's demise, Carter welcomed the Prime Minister of Thailand to the White House in February by saying that the United States was "deeply committed to the integrity and to the freedom and the security of Thailand—that your borders stay inviolate," a pledge he backed with transfers of equipment and ammunition during the next Vietnamese offensive in Cambodia.[3] Meanwhile, the administration not only completed full diplomatic recognition of China but gave the rapprochement a strongly strategic cast, by offering dual-use technology and nonlethal military equipment, and by sending Secretary of Defense Harold Brown to Peking to endorse "wider cooperation on security matters" and "complementary actions in the field of defense as well as diplomacy."[4] Though the security treaty with Taiwan had to be terminated in the process, the Taiwan Relations Act initiated by the Congress more than reaffirmed the unilateral U.S. commitment, declaring that the United States would maintain the capacity to resist any coercion jeopardizing the island's security and would consider the use of force against it as a matter of "grave concern" and a "threat to the peace."[5] At the same time the United States began publicly to push Japan for more defense spending and to support diplomatic unity and military cooperation among ASEAN states, while also concluding a half-billion dollar deal to retain its bases in the Philippines.

In late 1979 and 1980 there was also a change in the Carter administration's reluctance to maintain old or undertake new commitments in Africa. While in 1977 and 1978 Carter had finessed invasions of Zaire's territory from Angola, having in mind the incompetence and corruption of Mobutu Sese Seko's regime, by 1979 the administration was putting its emphasis on helping to modernize the dictator's army. Now eager to demonstrate U.S. support for a long time American ally under attack, the President also decided in October 1979 to sell counterinsurgency weaponry to Morocco's King Hassan for use against the Polisario guerrillas in the Western Sahara. Similarly, in February 1980 the administration rushed to provide military equipment to Tunisia after a Libyan-sponsored raid on its border town of Gafsa, even though the United States had no formal commitment to the North African country.[6]

But the most dramatic and significant extension of U.S. security commitments during the later Carter years was in the Middle East. One part of the administration's expansion of security ties there came out of its Camp David peacemaking effort, which demanded extensive U.S. financial and security commitments to Egypt and Israel. For Egypt, the United States initiated a massive arms supply relationship, envisioning a $2.5–$6 billion investment during the first half of the eighties. For Israel, new security guarantees were given, including the positioning of U.S. technicians in tripwire position in the Sinai (providing Israel with what Moshe Dayan called "the shield of the United States"), as well as written promises to make up shortfalls in oil supplies. In addition, a Memorandum of Understanding attached to the Egyptian-Israeli peace treaty pledged the United States, in case of a treaty violation threatening Israel's security, to take appropriate "remedial measures" (including military action) and urgently to consider ending the violation by strengthening the U.S. presence in the area, providing emergency military supplies, or exercising the U.S. maritime rights.[7]

The other and more impressive part of the Carter Middle East policy involved the extension of American commitment to a "region" the administration itself conjured up for the purpose: Southwest Asia. U.S. involvement there came in three overlapping stages as the crisis deepened and the requirements of commitment became clearer. First, Carter moved in the immediate aftermath of the Shah's fall to reassure moderate Arab regimes, particularly Saudi Arabia. In February 1979 Secretary Brown visited Riyadh to promise "training and equipment better than any in the world" and pledge that the United States would stand by its friends in peace or war, while in March Secretary of State Cyrus Vance affirmed that the United States considered "the territorial integrity and security of Saudi Arabia a matter of fundamental interest."[8] To make those pledges real, the administration provided military aid totalling over $380 million to North Yemen when it was attacked by South Yemen, and Carter sent AWACS early warning aircraft to help protect Saudi Arabia against foreign intrusion in March 1979 and again at the outbreak of the Iran-Iraq conflict in October 1980.[9]

Such pledges forced the administration to do some hard thinking about the projection of military power into the region, and the second part of its growing commitment to Southwest Asia involved an increase in American forces there. Following a critical series of policy review meetings in June 1979, the United States gradually increased its military presence to 20–30 warships (including two aircraft carriers), a Marine Amphibious Unit of 1,800 men, and land-based tactical fighter squadrons on frequent exercise/assistance missions.[10] In addition, the Rapid

Deployment Force was created to maximize deployable U.S.-based assets; by mid-1980 some 200,000 active and 100,000 reserve forces were earmarked for the RDF, whose equipment was being prepositioned on 15 cargo ships in the Indian Ocean. All of this was to back up a tripwire strategy of preemptive deterrence, whereby the United States would put American troops on the ground quickly in case of Soviet attack or threatened attack, dramatically raising the stakes of Soviet adventurism and with them, presumably, the power of American deterrence.[11]

But the United States could not seriously challenge Soviet military power 12,000 miles away with a few ships and a lightly-armed RDF; much more would be needed for real defense. Hence, the third and most committing part of the Carter strategy was the diplomatic effort to acquire enroute and in-area basing for large, "surge" deployments of U.S. forces. Here the administration faced a dilemma. However much the Pentagon might want U.S.-owned or controlled bases for their forces, and however much local leaders might want a physical presence to offset their concern about American reliability and steadfastness, there was no question in the 1980s of recreating the kind of base structure that once supported the Dulles alliances. Fearing the fate of the Shah, the rulers of Southwest Asia could not afford open identification with the superpower which armed and bankrolled Israel, nor would they welcome being caught in a superpower cross fire on their territory.

So instead of requesting bases, the Carter administration began in 1979 asking selected states on the Indian Ocean littoral whether they would make their facilities available to U.S. forces for peacetime training and crisis deployments. In return, the United States would welcome them into a long-term security partnership, including extensive, American-funded expansion and improvements to their facilities, continuing economic and military aid, and—significantly—express or implied assurances of U.S. intent to protect them against outside attack. Everything would be very discreet: no formal treaties were envisioned, host country control would be retained, and the peacetime American presence at each location would be kept at austere levels.

Working under this formula, U.S. negotiating teams secured agreements in 1980 with Oman, Kenya, and Somalia.[12] Although the Saudis turned Harold Brown down flat when he suggested a U.S. base on their territory in February 1979, Anwar Sadat authorized construction of a "nonbase" at Ras Banas on the Red Sea able to accommodate the deployment of 18,000 men and handle the most sophisticated U.S. aircraft.[13] The Carter administration also began consultations with allies enroute to the Persian Gulf, including Morocco and members of NATO and the ANZUS, for use of their facilities during a crisis deployment to the area.

President Carter capped these preparations with the enunciation of a "doctrine" reminiscent of those bearing the names of the earlier alliance builders, Truman and Eisenhower: a pledge that the United States would repel, if necessary by military force, any outside attempt "to gain control of the Persian Gulf region." And by the time he left office in January 1981, the United States had gone a considerable distance towards making that promise real, in the process acquiring a new and growing set of security relationships with a very different group of Third World states. It had also improvised a new way of forging security commitments without formal treaties or bases, one more in tune with a post-colonial world overseas and a post-Vietnam world at home. The new set of U.S. commitments would be cemented by facilities access agreements and follow-on construction investments, military assistance and arms sales, high-level political visits and assurances. It was a modus operandi which Carter's successor would adopt with a vengeance.

THE REAGAN ADAPTATION: DOGMA OVER DOCTRINE

For all its boldness and success in expanding U.S. security commitments in the Third World, the Carter administration acted in response to events, more out of necessity than conviction. But for the Reagan administration, strengthening and expanding American alliances has been a mission proceeding from dogma, a critical element in its intended restoration of American power. In fact, Ronald Reagan sees strong security commitments as an essential instrument in the struggle against the overwhelming threat posed by the Soviet Union. As he put it in a 1983 address to the American Legion, "Maintenance of our alliance partnerships is a key to our foreign policy."[14]

The role of Third World security commitments in the restoration of American power appears in administration thinking on several levels. First, alliances are seen in their traditional role as a tool that can aggregate the military power of the free world for deterrence or defense. If the whole is stronger than the sum of its parts, then presumably those portions of the Third World sympathetic to the West will be more able to resist Soviet political or military encroachment—and Moscow will be better deterred from pressuring them—if they are tied to and fortified by the United States. Nor is the administration unmindful of the important function these alliances play in the projection of the United States' *own* military power. As Secretary of State George Shultz put it in 1983, "The United States cannot defend its interests by operating out of the United States and Europe alone. We need the cooperation of countries in the Third World to grant transit, refueling, and base rights."[15] Here the commitment process tends to interact with the Reagan defense buildup. Greatly expanded U.S. military forces are considered necessary to support new allies; but the bigger, more deployable forces also need more enroute access, more in-area facilities, more overseas training and exercising—each in itself a committing activity that tends to create new security partners whose defense demands still more American military forces.

But conservatives in and out of the Reagan administration connect support of Third World allies to the restoration of American power in more profound and complex ways, many of them, ironically, related to the Reagan indictment of the administration which started the recommitment process. When first accepting his party's nomination for president, Reagan condemned his predecessor's as an "amateurish and confused Administration" whose weakness and vacillation had led U.S. allies to "reluctantly conclude that America is unwilling or unable to fulfill its obligations as leader of the free world," thus undermining the psychological basis of American power.[16] In fact, Reagan believed that the Shah and Somoza would have not fallen but for lack of firm U.S. support; as president, he argued that if the United States would "make it plain . . . that we are going to stand by our friends and allies" like Israel, Egypt, and the Sudan [sic], no "overthrow would take place."[17] Accordingly, President Reagan assured American allies in his first Inaugural Address "of our support and firm commitment. We will match," he said, "loyalty with loyalty."

U.S. support of allies abroad thus became an article of faith with the new administration. The viciously anti-American nature of Khomeini's regime in Iran and the Sandinistas' links with Havana and Moscow led conservatives like Jean Kirkpatrick to advance as a general proposition the idea that the United States should cement its security relationships with authoritarian regimes, however distasteful, rather than risk the rise of totalitarian governments which might become allied to the Soviet Union. Though liberals might recoil at the implications of such a policy, many conservatives found the real ethical issue not in the purity of the regimes with which the United States might be associated but in the sanctity of American promises. For them, maintaining one's alliances was a matter of national honor; "international divorce" of the kind necessitated by Jimmy Carter's recognition of China at Taiwan's expense posed serious questions of morality. Such concerns put an ideological edge on the more practical considerations of high administration officials.

Indeed, the Reagan administration has acted as though the necessity of recruiting and supporting allies in the struggle against the Soviet Union outweighs virtually all other considerations in its Third World policy. As we have noted, the Carter administration began life committed to a set of goals in the Third World which seemed in the short run to frustrate close security ties with many allied regimes. First, American support for *human rights* soured relations with South Korea and many Latin American governments. Second, Carter's *nuclear nonproliferation* effort offended would-be nuclear powers in the Third World; in Pakistan, for example, it resulted in a total cutoff of assistance in April 1979, rupturing the relationship so badly that President Zia contemptuously rejected the $400 million in U.S. aid Carter offered after the Soviet invasion of Afghanistan. Third, the Carter administration's determination to *restrict arms transfers* deprived the United States of one of the critical tools of commitment formation. Although Carter had begun to back away from all three goals as his recommitment effort began in 1979, their residue in the bureaucracy and in legislation continued to exert a powerful effect on his administration's diplomacy.

The Reagan team quite explicitly lowered the priority of all these objectives when it came into office. It determined to pursue human rights through quiet diplomacy, and quickly reestablished security relationships with Argentina, Brazil, Chile, and other offending Latin American states.[18] It discarded restraints on arms transfers as an "escape from reality" that "substituted theology for a healthy sense of self-preservation," and has increased not only the volume but also the sophistication of arms transfers to security partners in the Third World, including top-of-the-line aircraft and the latest missiles.[19] The priority of nonproliferation was also lowered, and changes in U.S. law were sought to make possible a 5-year, $3.2 billion assistance package which Pakistan *did* accept in 1981, including 40 F-16 fighters with full equipment packages and the latest Sidewinder air-to-air missiles.[20] As a result, the administration was able to add a refurbished alliance with Pakistan (under a 1959 defense cooperation agreement left over from the Dulles era) to its commitments in Southwest Asia.

Single-mindedness in the anti-Soviet struggle has also affected U.S. commitments in the Third World because of the administration's determination to actively oppose Soviet proxy states like Cuba, Libya, Nicaragua, and Vietnam. Reagan's escalating pressure against Libya has been a major factor in the expansion of American commitments to its neighbors (Tunisia and the Sudan, in particular), and it has also affected relations with Egypt (which the United States apparently tried to recruit for joint attack on Libya).[21] Similarly, American opposition to Cuban expansion has meant increased involvement in Eastern Caribbean and, of course, Central American security matters. Most important, execution of the so-called Reagan doctrine—providing material support to armed insurgencies fighting Soviet-backed regimes in Nicaragua, Afghanistan, Cambodia, and Angola—has required greatly strengthened U.S. commitments to those Third World allies from whose territory the "freedom fighters" operate, especially Honduras, Pakistan, and Thailand.

Indeed, for an administration preoccupied by the struggle with the "evil empire,"[22] security commitments in the Third World ultimately must seem more than a useful weapon, more critical than even a vital means to an end. For if the Third World is the battleground in the East-West struggle, and if Third World states are the stakes of combat, then security relationships ultimately become an essential part of keeping score in the geopolitical game[23]—they go a long way towards defining whose side a country is on and hence who is winning or losing the global contest. Propelled by the logic of its convictions, it is hardly surprising that the Reagan administration has gone far beyond President Carter's limited efforts to deal with a world that so disappointed his original expectations.

NEW COMMITMENT TECHNIQUES

In fact, the Reagan administration has utilized and expanded most of the Carter commitment techniques while inventing a few of its own. First, the administration has more than followed through on the Carter facilities access efforts, emplacing substantial military investments in the Persian Gulf and around the world. Fifty to sixty million dollar construction programs have been completed at Mombassa in Kenya and at Berbera naval base in Somalia, and over $300 million has been spent for ongoing improvements at four airfields in Oman. Moving beyond the Carter framework, the administration obtained written access in 1982 to selected Moroccan airfields for emergency transit and periodic training of U.S. forces, and it has spent $5 million improving Sidi Sliman airbase near Casablanca.[24] Also, it was reportedly able in 1984 to get Saudi Arabia's agreement to U.S. use of its facilities in case of Soviet aggression or a regional crisis beyond the Kingdom's control.[25] All these facilities are for the use of the Rapid Deployment Force, upgraded in 1983 into a "Central Command" like those the Pentagon has maintained for years in the Atlantic, Pacific, and Southern Hemisphere, and now boasting of 300,000 earmarked forces, a U.S.-based planning staff, a forward headquarters afloat in the Persian Gulf, and the experience of some combined exercises with host country forces.[26]

While expanding U.S. access and facilities in Southwest Asia along lines laid out by its predecessor, the Reagan administration has pioneered a slightly different commitment technique in Central America. Here, since 1983, the United States has mounted a virtually continuous series of large-scale exercises and military maneuvers, involving from 350 to 5,000 U.S. troops, often in conjunction with Honduran forces. Many of these exercises left behind millions of dollars in infrastructure, including wells, roads, bridges, airstrips, and radars, leading some Democratic congressmen to charge that the administration was using them as an end run around the usual procedures for appropriating military construction funds. The United States also maintains some 800 to 1,600 U.S. troops on six-months rotation at Palmerola Air Base (where the American headquarters for Honduras is located) and around the country.[27] The immediate purpose of this presence is to provide real-time intelligence to the Salvadoran armed forces and the contras, but administration civilians say it is also intended as a kind of guarantee to Honduras.[28] Although the administration refused the Hondurans' request in 1984 for a binding treaty of alliance, President Reagan made the U.S. commitment explicit in 1985 by promising that the United States would provide "timely and effective" support to Honduras' "efforts to defend its sovereignty and territorial integrity" in case of "armed attack" by "Communist" forces.[29]

The Reagan administration has also been far more vigorous than its predecessor in using security assistance to cement Third World defense ties. While Carter was an economic internationalist committed to Third World development and to the use of economic assistance to meet basic human needs, the Reagan administration believes in nationalist economic premises and is convinced that Third World development can come only from entrepreneurial, free market strategies, with outside help mainly in the form of private investment. Hence, the administration has felt free to shift the emphasis in U.S. foreign assistance away from development projects to military equipment and training. From 1980 to 1986, U.S. economic assistance (bilateral and multilateral) actually declined 8 percent while security assistance rose 130 percent; grants of military equipment to U.S. allies have increased some 600 percent in the same period.[30] Major increases (of from 50 percent to 100 percent) have been provided to Morocco, the Sudan, Somalia, Óman, and South Korea, and huge increases (100 percent up to 3,000 percent) to Egypt, Pakistan, Thailand, El Salvador, Honduras, and Tunisia, often in the context of facilities access or base agreement negotiations.[31]

Another technique in the Reagan administration commitment policy has been U.S. support of regional alliances, as modern proxies for the direct multilateral commitments of the Dulles era. One good example is the Association of Southeast Asian Nations (ASEAN), left as the only formal grouping in that region after the demise of SEATO. ASEAN is ostensibly an economic pact, but its members' economies are competitive rather than complementary (only 10 percent of their trade is internal), and the organization was founded in 1967 and energized after 1975 for geopolitical and defense reasons. Beginning in the late 1970s and continuing into the early 1980s, Thailand, Indonesia, Malaysia, and Singapore have dramatically increased their defense spending and intensified their bilateral military cooperation; today they exchange intelligence, patrol jointly against insurgencies, and regularly exercise their naval forces.[32] The last two countries are also the beneficiaries of defense assistance from Australia, New Zealand, and the UK through the Five Power Defense Agreements of 1971, to which the United States is connected through the ANZUS and NATO treaties. Given all these practical and legal ties, one could easily argue that ASEAN is becoming a strategic entity whose military cooperation falls just short of a collective defense effort.[33]

Although not a member of ASEAN, the United States strongly supports it on political, economic, and military levels. First, of course, the United States has direct legal commitments to defend two of its six members, Thailand, and the Philippines. In addition, U.S. arms sales to ASEAN states jumped from $916 million during the mid-1970s (1972–78) to $3.37 billion during the comparable Carter/Reagan (1979–85) period; some 60 percent of these have been to Thailand, where the United States has recently concluded agreements to stockpile equipment and (in March 1985) offered to sell F-16s.[34] This concrete support has been reinforced by the now-routine attendance of the U.S. Secretary of State at the June meetings of ASEAN foreign ministers, by President Reagan's 1986 meeting with the ASEAN heads of state in Indonesia, and by his 1982 statement that the United States will "never lose sight of ASEAN's concerns, or neglect our commitments to the ASEAN countries."[35]

Another proxy alliance supported by the Reagan administration is the Gulf Cooperation Council, a defensive grouping of the smaller Persian Gulf sheikdoms (including Kuwait, Bahrain, Qatar, the UAE, and Oman) formed around Saudi Arabia after the outbreak of the Iran-Iraq war. Although the United States has no formal ties to any of these states (except the facilities access agreement with Oman), American support for this overtly military organization is again very clear. In the first place, President Reagan has not only endorsed the

Carter Doctrine but expanded it to include internal threats to Gulf regimes: "I have to say that . . . we will not permit [Saudi Arabia] to be an Iran."[36] Furthermore, the whole of CENTCOM is oriented towards defending these countries; its forward headquarters is at Bahrain, already host to the five ships of the U.S. Navy's Middle East Force. Moreover, the administration's sale to Saudi Arabia, after a long and difficult congressional struggle in 1981–82, of five AWACS aircraft was the key part of a $4 billion integrated air defense system for these countries.[37] For fiscal years 1981–85, in fact, the United States sold nearly $15 billion in arms to the GCC ($13 billion of it to the Saudis), and provided over $125 million in military assistance to Oman.[38]

The administration has also attempted to support local defense groupings closer to home. Although its 1983 effort to revitalize the Central American Defense Council (CONDECA) for use against Nicaragua failed,[39] the United States has spent some $20–30 million arming and training Special Service Units in Eastern Caribbean police forces with the objective of creating a mutual defense organization known as the Regional Security System. Policemen from St. Lucia, St. Vincent and the Grenadines, St. Christopher-Nevis, Dominica, and Granada, as well as the military forces of Antigua, Barbuda and Barbados are involved, and some 120 of them had their first exercise with U.S. forces in September 1985.[40] Of even greater interest is the fact that it was the Organization of Eastern Caribbean States that requested American intervention in Granada in the fall of 1983.

The Reagan administration, then, has expanded U.S. security commitments in the Third World through facilities' access arrangements, military construction, arms transfers and security assistance, support of regional security arrangements, political cooperation, joint planning and exercising, and explicit promises to defend. In addition and informing them all, the administration has created expectations of U.S. commitment by its manifest determination to defend all nations threatened by the Soviet Union or its clients. If the Nixon Doctrine devalued U.S. commitments by withholding the use of American combat forces, and the Carter Doctrine extended to a new region the protection of an administration whose resolve was widely disparaged, the real "Reagan doctrine" is perhaps the administration's demonstrated willingness to provide emergency assistance and even use force to protect Third World allies. Aid was dispatched to Chad and AWACS to the Sudan when Libya threatened, emergency supplies have repeatedly been flown to Thailand when Vietnamese forces overran the Cambodian border, and $20 million in supplies were sent to Honduras when the Sandinistas attacked contra camps in that country—even though Tegucigalpa preferred not to acknowledge the attack.[41] Of greatest symbolic importance,

Reagan has twice shown himself willing to authorize direct military attacks on Soviet clients, regardless of adverse reaction. Such actions inevitably reinforce the ties formed by the more subtle techniques discussed above.

LIABILITIES OF THE NEW COMMITMENT STRUCTURE

What, then, is the shape of the Carter/Reagan set of security commitments in the Third World? Or more broadly, what is the structure of American security commitments there after this third wave of commitment formation? For what exists today are remnants of the Dulles, treaty-based system overlaid by the very different ties formed in the last eight years. What are the implications of those differences, and of a commitment structure which combines both formal and informal security relationships, for U.S. national security policy in the years ahead?

Compared with the U.S. alliance system of 25 years ago, the current structure of security relationships seems far less than ideal. In the first place, it is much less intensive and less geographically contiguous, clearly incapable of any peripheral, military containment of the Soviet Union. Where once the Asian bilateral treaties, SEATO and CENTO, made an unbroken line from Japan through Southeast and South Asia and the Middle East to NATO, there are now Soviet-backed Syria, Khomeini's Iran, Soviet-occupied Afghanistan, and Vietnamese-controlled Indochina with Soviet bases at Danang and Cam Rahn Bay. On the other hand, of course, the Soviet blue-water navy and growing airlift capability would make perimeter containment difficult in any case. And the transformation of China from one of those being contained into at least a formidable strategic buffer is a shift of enormous positive significance.

But even if one considers the new alliance system as suitable to strongpoint rather than perimeter defense, there are still serious problems. Compared with the Truman/Acheson and even the Eisenhower/Dulles system, the Carter/Reagan security relationships are pale alliances which hardly seem to deserve the name. The lack of formal treaty ties, the extreme political discretion with which these relationships must be handled, the inability to station U.S. forces permanently in most of these countries, let alone in tripwire positions, all suggest that these states should be thought of not as allies but "coalites"—partners in security coalitions with the United States. Under such circumstances, the commitment is less clearly established and any defense would be far more difficult; hence, the deterrence in most cases must be far less effective.

Moreover, it is difficult to believe that the current set of Third World commitments is very successful at aggregating free world power. Not only is the summation of the parts less accomplished, but like the Dulles system before it, the Carter/Reagan allies themselves can add little to American power. In fact, the building blocks of this alliance system are so weak that they absorb resources rather than contributing them, while at the same time the new relationships vastly expand the area American power is committed to defend. Although this was somewhat true of the Dulles system as well, the United States today produces less than half the percentage of gross world product that it captured in the 1950s and is therefore far less able to support far-flung commitments. Instead of aggregating power, then, the Carter/Reagan commitments add to the problem of solvency that faces American policymakers with increasing urgency. As proof, one need go no farther than the plight of foreign aid for FY 1987 under the Gramm-Rudman-Hollings law, where few funds will be left to support foreign policy beyond the amounts pledged to U.S. Camp David allies and to states still providing American bases and facilities.

It is true, of course, that many of the Carter/Reagan commitments came into existence neither for perimeter military containment nor to aggregate power for deterrence and defense. Many recent commitments have been made, as we have seen, simply to acquire rights necessary for power projection by American forces or to provide platforms for armed insurgencies directed against Soviet client states. Indeed, the secondary nature of most of these commitments seems even more obvious than for those of John Foster Dulles. Like his alliances, some of the Carter/Reagan commitments were initiated to respond to local crises (like the fall of Iran and the invasion of Afghanistan); they hardly seem integral parts of a sophisticated strategy. Most, in fact, seem to extend American protection—as payment for services rendered—to areas not of importance for any other reason, leading to a certain imbalance (from the American point of view) between the immediate benefit and the potential cost. Alliances should always be seen as means to an end—the end being U.S. national security—never as ends in themselves. Many of these pacts strike one as means to a means, leaving one to wonder whether the promise of protection would ever be fulfilled.

In this regard, the use of allies under the Reagan doctrine requires particular caution. Whatever the value of supporting armed insurgencies, these operations pose special dangers for nations like Honduras, Pakistan, and Thailand from whose territory they operate. That their leaders recognize this danger is clear from General Zia's refusal to accept a mere $400 million from the Carter administration, or from

Honduras' frantic effort to get a mutual defense treaty from the Reagan administration. Ironically, the danger is in direct proportion to the involvement of powerful patrons on the other side, particularly the USSR, which means it is greatest in precisely those cases where there is the strongest domestic support in the United States for intervention. If, for example, Pakistan is attacked by Soviet/Afghan forces, American prestige will be unequivocably engaged, and the result will be an extraordinarily dangerous situation, not just for the United States, but for the world.

Considerations such as those raised above are not the only reasons one may question the stability of the Carter/Reagan commitment tier. As the fate of the Dulles system has shown, the cultural dissimilarity and extreme fragility of many Third World regimes predisposes any West-South alliance relationship to instability; how much more must this be true in relationships without treaties, without the presence of U.S. forces, and where the promise to defend is backed by so little apparent national interest? The Sudan has already provided one instance, and the Philippines nearly another, for the administration to ponder. Moreover, the Reagan approach to Third World security commitments seems to produce alliance relationships that are particularly vulnerable to decay, in spite of—or indeed, ironically, because of—its very stress on security commitments. This is true in at least two fundamental ways.

In the first place, the administration's downplaying of secondary goals like arms transfer restraint, nuclear nonproliferation, and human rights because they antagonized some allied governments during the Carter years may well come back to weaken or even destroy the very security relationships being cultivated. The Philippines, again, provided a near example of what can happen when human rights are neglected: government brutality, uncorrected, helped cause a manageable insurgency to grow into a serious insurrection that may yet destroy the regime which the downplaying of the human rights policy was designed to preserve. If change did not come too late in the Philippines, South Korea and Zaire are perhaps the most obvious next candidates. In the case of nonproliferation, one can well imagine what effect a Pakistani nuclear test (after the last of the F-16 enhancements are delivered) would have on Congress' willingness to vote continued military aid. Uncontrolled arms transfers pose similar dangers, particularly in the Middle East, but anywhere the growing numbers and sophistication of armaments lend more intense destruction to the next war and increase the chance that an American coalite will find itself in serious trouble.

In the second place, many of the administration's specific policies are producing a growing alienation in the Third World in general (and among certain groups of allied nations in particular) from the United States. Unlike its predecessor, the Reagan administration is seen as prejudiced against many traditional Third World causes. It is skeptical of development aid, was rather negative about the international financial institutions, left UNESCO and took a tough stance at the UN, refused to agree to the Law of the Sea Treaty. Moreover, it is often perceived to be on the wrong side (from the LDC point of view) of local or regional political issues, for example the black/white issue in Southern Africa or arming the contras against Nicaragua in Central America. At the September 1986 meeting of the Non-Aligned Movement in Zimbabwe, these policies produced draft declarations containing 54 explicit attacks on the United States, compared with only 14 at the 1980 Havana summit chaired by Fidel Castro—hardly a friend of the United States.[42]

One good example of the perils of political heavy-handedness is in the Far East: the PRC-Taiwan problem. Pro-Taiwan conservatives tried very hard during the transition period to commit the administration to making U.S. ties to Taiwan official, and their success in pressing for arms sales to the island threw U.S.-PRC relations into a deep freeze during the first year and a half of the Reagan era. But the strategic consequences of reversing the rapprochement with China, pursued for a dozen years by three administrations of both political parties, were so horrific that in August 1982 the administration signed a communique with Beijing regulating the arms sales question. As a result the U.S.-PRC relationship has developed into a proto-alliance featuring intelligence sharing, military sales, and naval visits. However, transfers since late 1984 of technology needed for Taiwan to produce an Indigenous Defensive Fighter may yet again threaten the course of the Sino-American entente.

But perhaps the most obvious example of the damaging effect of political complications on security commitments is in the Middle East and Southwest Asia, where a variety of disintegrative forces are beginning already to corrupt the new commitments of the Carter/Reagan era. Whatever its success with facilities access and the Gulf Cooperation Council, the most noteworthy Reagan contribution to U.S. commitments there has been the deepening relationship with Israel. Although at first relations were strained by Tel Aviv's annexation of the Golan Heights and invasion of Lebanon, the American-Israeli alliance was strengthened by a strategic cooperation agreement originally signed in November 1981 and revived in November 1983. The agreement's public provisions established a joint military committee and envisioned combined planning, joint maneuvers, and stockpiling of U.S. equipment in Israel,[43] and shortly after its signing President Reagan again put on record his "unswerving commitment" to Israel's security.[44] Subsequent years have seen dramatically increased and liberalized American aid, as well as the unprecedented establishment in 1985 of a U.S.-Israeli free trade zone.

In the context of the administration's failure to make substantial progress in the Arab-Israeli peace process, however, the closer U.S. identification with Israel has considerably offset Reagan's efforts to strengthen defense ties with the moderate Arabs. Egypt under Hosni Mubarak is a case in point. Angered by the Israeli invasion of Lebanon, increasingly frustrated with U.S. inability or unwillingness to bring Israel to the peace table, eager to repair relations with its Arab neighbors, and fearful of growing dependence on the United States (and of the mounting debt occasioned by military purchases), Cairo froze relations with Tel Aviv until the Perez-Mubarak summit of September 1986 and cancelled American construction of the Ras Banas base, becoming far more defensive about overt politico-military cooperation with Washington.[45] Similar damaging effects are evident in American security relations to Jordan, where King Hussein has repeatedly cited American refusal to deliver Israel as reason for his own repeated failures to move the Palestinian problem towards a settlement. Although the administration has continued to provide massive assistance to Egypt under the Camp David formula and has more than doubled military assistance to Jordan, it is unlikely that these technical relationships can overcome continuing political frustration.[46]

Indeed, lack of the kind of progress President Carter was able to produce in the Arab-Israeli dispute has served to weaken U.S. security ties to the moderate Arabs in yet another way, perversely, through the reflection of their dissatisfaction with the United States in the American political process. Because there are no formal alliances in the Middle East left over from the Truman or Eisenhower eras, the Carter/Reagan security commitments there are even more than ordinarily dependent on arms sales. The clout of Israel's supporters in the American political process makes such sales to, for example, the Saudis difficult even in the best of times; Carter's 1978 F-15 sale and the Reagan 1982 AWACS sale were among the toughest for each administration to get through Congress. When moderate Arabs criticize the United States for its support of an aggressive Israel—or, more recently, for its own military retaliations against Arab terrorism—securing congressional consent for these sales becomes nearly impossible. Thus, after a long delay, Reagan had to withdraw a request to sell Stinger missiles to Jordan in 1984 after the King bitterly criticized the United States as an unreliable partner in the peace process. In 1985 and 1986, another Jordanian package was cancelled and a Saudi package emasculated when humiliating congressional defeat seemed unavoidable. The result was that the Saudis bought 72 Toronado fighters from the UK, while the Jordanians acquired their "stingers" from the USSR.[47]

Meanwhile, the underlying motivation for American commitments in the area seems to be subtly shifting from the days of the Carter Doctrine. Although it is still of vital importance to America's European allies, Middle Eastern oil has gradually become far less critical to the U.S. economy; the glut and massive price drops beginning in the winter of 1985–86 only serve to further weaken America's perceived interest in the Gulf. At the same time, the U.S. concern with terrorism and its efforts to isolate Qadaffi's Libya (and protect nations around it from Libyan aggression) has shifted policymakers' attention while Arab connections to terrorist activities have subtly discredited all Arab regimes. Certainly terrorism and Libya are of concern to its neighbors—particularly Tunisia, Chad, and Egypt—but that does not mean they support American ways of dealing with it, as Egypt's rejection of U.S. plans to invade Libya and her anger at the American's capture of the *Achille Lauro* hijackers demonstrates. Nor does it mean the United States will be successful in building coalitions to contain Qadaffi, as King Hassan's political union with Tripoli and the fall of Jaafar Nimeiri's government in the Sudan show.

There is one final consideration which should be borne in mind when analyzing the Reagan commitment policy. Based as it is on a zero-sum view of geopolitics in the Soviet struggle, the new system has the effect of accentuating—one might say perpetuating—the bipolar nature of the international political system. Like Dulles before it, it rests on the intrinsic premise that any state not with the United States is against it, that "neutralism is immoral." In so doing, it puts the United States in a position where it must ultimately prepare either to oppose a hundred enemies or support a hundred allies, failing apparently to recognize that Americans can no more afford the latter than the former. In 1914, opposed alliance systems helped push the world towards war. In the 1900s, the dictates of nuclear peace (if not fiscal constraints alone) may well demand a broader solution.

THE FUTURE OF COMMITMENT IN AMERICAN FOREIGN POLICY

Do these problems admit of any answers? Or are the Carter/Reagan commitments the best one can do in the current situation?

As their being products of two fundamentally different administrations might suggest, it is important to recognize that many of the shortcomings of this third wave of commitment formation are unavoidable. We are unlikely to return to the era of formal, treaty-based alliances. Third World states will continue to be fragile, their leaders wary of overt connection to a foreign power, especially a superpower. The problems decisionmakers face in creating deterrence in an era when the tools of commitment are in short supply are likely to multiply, as are the problems of projecting American military power. Indeed, with base costs escalating, with fewer and fewer locations available, and with less and less control over facilities being granted, the tendency will be to extend commitment to more and more marginal countries in order to secure the capability to defend the areas that really count.

Some critics argue that the paradigm of deterrence through alliance which has characterized postwar policy since at least 1948 has run its course, that a radically new approach is needed. And yet, the Truman/ Acheson alliances continue to serve the country well; few would willingly abandon NATO, the treaty with Japan, or even the ANZUS alliance. The problem rather lies in application of the paradigm, and perhaps the solution can be found in recalling the concept of alliance used in earlier days, in seeing commitments as part of a sophisticated national security strategy.

First, new U.S. security commitments must be set in the context of a policy which understands not only the Soviet threat but also the broader political terrain on which the contest is being waged. Washington must not lose sight of the fact that its position on general Third World concerns, its stance on local political issues, and the perceived vigor of its diplomacy in addressing regional conflicts is of vital importance in the success of its coalition-building efforts. In global geopolitics, single-mindedness is not necessarily the surest route to success; goals which may seem peripheral can often be critical over the long run.

Second, administrations of both parties must be more careful in choosing the objects to which they pledge, implicitly and explicitly, this country's defense. A closer definition of what Bernard Brodie called "the outer limits of the truly vital" in the Third World, one that takes account of the real complementarity of interest and likelihood of at least mid-term stability among prospective American coalites, would help to mitigate the intrinsic disadvantage of commitments in the South. If American resources are limited, it would seem prudent to concentrate them on new allies more like the Truman than Dulles partners, those which can really help aggregate power or which at least have some prospect of doing so down the road.

Third, while thus making security demands less extensive, future administrations can and should make them less intensive as well. The mistaken tendency to offer commitment as payment for some perceived U.S. security "need" can be much attenuated if American security requirements themselves are reduced. In Central America, for example, the United States need not demand a fully democratic political system or even a reduction in the Sandinista army in order to meet its real security needs; all a minimum definition of American security requires is a promise by Managua to stop the export of revolutionary arms and not to emplace Soviet offensive weapons on Nicaraguan soil. Achieving a settlement along those lines would much reduce both the danger of, and the occasion for, U.S. commitment to Honduras.

Of course, such suggestions will seem hopelessly naive to anyone who thinks in zero-sum, bipolar terms, who assumes that security in the Third World must be created in each instance by American power and will. And indeed, none of the arguments advanced above can possibly be accepted unless one also entertains the possibility that some of the changes in the Third World since Dulles' time can be beneficial in terms of American security, that the very currents of greater independence and maturity which so often seem to frustrate American control in the South might work to our benefit.

Recently, the idea of the United States as a champion of democracy abroad has come increasingly into focus. If applied in anything but an exhortative fashion, this is surely a recipe for endless meddling in the internal systems of other states, for a recklessly intensive definition of American security needs. Instead, the United States should champion democracy at the systemic level, adopting an explicitly pluralistic security policy that would in effect make the world safe for neutralism. It is not the United States, after all, but the Soviet Union whose ideology demands that all nations be made over in its image; we should support an international system of different states living in peaceful relations with one another. Such a policy would attempt to widen the space in between the superpowers, encouraging self-reliance outside their spheres of influence and reserving the tools of commitment for those who can genuinely help maintain those systemic ideals.

The Reagan administration has made a few moves in line with such an approach. Neutralist Chadli Benjedid of Algeria was entertained at the White House in 1985, as was marxist Samora Machel of Mozambique. But more than gestures are needed. For it is likely that resource constraints and the growing competence of Third World states as they move beyond their third decade of independence will push the United States towards a pluralistic policy anyway. It may even be, irony of ironies, that such an approach would be the best way to strengthen those commitments of greatest and enduring value.

NOTES

1. This article was written during a recent sabbatical as Resident Associate at the Carnegie Endowment for International Peace; an abridged version appears in *Foreign Policy* magazine (No. 67, Summer 1987). The views expressed here are the author's own and do not necessarily reflect those of the U.S. Government or any of its agencies.

2. Quoted in *Washington Post* (July 1, 1979).

3. Quoted in *Washington Post* (February 7, 1979).

4. Philip Geyelin, "Arms Sales: The China Differential," *Washington Post* (May 23, 1980); Brown quoted in *Washington Post* (January 7, 1980).

5. Act of April 10, 1979, 22 USC 3301.

6. *Washington Post* (October 23, 1979, and February 1, 1980).

7. Egypt arms plans in *Washington Post* (February 11, 1979); Dayan quoted in *Washington Post* (September 27, 1979); M.O.U. text in *New York Times* (March 29, 1979).

8. Brown quoted in *Wall Street Journal* (February 16, 1979), and *Washington Post* (February 11, 1979); Vance CBS interview quoted in *Washington Post* (March 19, 1979).

9. Yemen decision in *Washington Post* (March 7, 1979); AWACS decision reported in *Washington Post* (March 9, 1979, and October 1, 1980).

10. *Washington Post* (July 1, 1979, and February 13, 1980).

11. *Washington Post* (February 2, June 19, August 7, 1980).

12. *Washington Post* (January 4, April 3, August 12 and 22, 1980).

13. Brown turndown, *New York Times* (February 27, 1979); Ras Banas, *Washington Post* (August 26, 1979).

14. Quoted from text in *Washington Post* (February 23, 1983), p. A12.

15. Address before the Southern Center for International Studies, Atlanta, Georgia (February 24, 1983), quoted in USAF *Selected Statements* 83–1 (January-March 1983), p. 76.

16. *Vital Speeches of the Day*, 46 (August 15, 1980), p. 645.

17. Text of luncheon meeting with newspaper editors in *New York Times* (October 18, 1981), p. 15.

18. Cynthia Gorney, "Reagan's Latin Policy," *Washington Post* (April 15, 1981), p. A25.

19. Undersecretary of State James Buckley, quoted in John Goshko, "Carter Restraints on Arms Sales to Friends Are Scrapped by Reagan Administration," *Washington Post* (May 22, 1981), p. A2.

20. Edward Walsh, "U.S. and Pakistan Agree on $3 Billion Aid Program," *Washington Post* (June 16, 1981), pp. A1, 12; Stuart Auerbach, "U.S. to Speed F16s as Pakistan Approves Aid," *Washington Post* (September 16, 1981), pp. A1, 16; Dana Adams Schmidt, "U.S. Gives Pakistan 40 F16s, Other Aid," *Times* (December 9, 1982), p. 5; David B. Ottaway, "U.S. Expediting Missiles for Pakistan's Defense," *Washington Post* (July 11, 1985).

21. Robert Woodward, "U.S. Unable to Persuade Egypt to Back Plans for Joint Anti-Qaddafi Move," *Washington Post* (April 2, 1986), pp. A1, 17.

22. Reagan speech of March 8, 1983, in Orlando, Florida.

23. Richard H. Ullman, "Containment and the Shape of World Politics," in Terry L. Deibel and John Lewis Gaddis, eds., *Containing the Soviet Union* (Washington: Pergamon-Brassey's, 1987).

24. "U.S. and Morocco Reach Accord on Use of Air Bases," *Washington Post* (May 28, 1982).

25. Bernard Gwertzman, "Saudis to Let U.S. Use Bases in Crisis," *New York Times* (September 5, 1985), pp. A1, 10.

26. Richard Halloran, "Poised for the Persian Gulf," *New York Times Magazine* (April 1, 1984), pp. 38–40, 61.

27. Fred Hiatt, "U.S. to Spend $50 Million to Build Honduras Facilities," "Entrenching in Honduras," *Washington Post* (February 7, 1986), pp. A1, 38 (February 18, 1986), pp. A1, 15.

28. Michael Getler, "Honduras Uneasy Over U.S. Military," *Washington Post* (April 7, 1985), p. A16.

29. Gerald M. Boyd, "Honduras Is Told U.S. Will Defend It," *New York Times* (May 22, 1985), p. 5.

30. Carol Lancaster, "The Budget and U.S. Foreign Aid: More Tough Choices?" *ODC Policy Focus*, No. 2 (Washington, DC: Overseas Development Council, February 1986), pp. 4–6. Figures are actual and estimated budget authority.

31. The figures, comparing FY 1980 to FY 1985, are as follows in millions of dollars: Morocco 25.9–49.5, Sudan 25.4–46.4, Somalia 20.4–34.1, Oman 25.0–40.2, Korea 130.5–231.9; Egypt .8–1176.7, Pakistan 0–326.0, Thailand 37.4–102.3, El Salvador 5.9–136.3, Honduras 3.9–67.4, Tunisia 15.6–66.6. *U.S. Overseas Loans and Grants* (Washington, DC: Agency for International Development, 1945–1980, 1985).

32. William T. Tow, "U.S. Alliance Policies and Asian-Pacific Security: A Transregional Approach," in Tow and William R. Feeney, eds., *U.S. Foreign Policy and Asian-Pacific Security* (Boulder, Colorado: Westview, 1982), pp. 37–46.

33. Justus M. van der Kroef, "ASEAN and U.S. Security Interests," *Strategic Review* 6 (Spring 1978), pp. 55–56.

34. Defense Security Assistance Agency, *Foreign Military Sales, Foreign Military Construction Sales, and Military Assistance Facts: As of September 30, 1985*, and *Foreign Military Sales and Military Assistance Facts: December 1979* (Washington, DC: Data Management Division, DSAA).

35. Richard M. Weintraub, "Ambassador to Indonesia Picked After Year's Delay," *Washington Post* (October 13, 1982).

36. News Conference of October 1, 1981, text in *New York Times* (October 2, 1981), pp. 1, 26.

37. Elaine Sciolino, "Saudis to Install $4 Billion Air Defense System," *New York Times* (May 19, 1985), p. 6.

38. George C. Wilson, "U.S. and Saudi Arabia Agree to Cooperate on Aid and Defense Planning," *Washington Post* (February 10, 1982), p. A19.

39. Jeff Gerth, "Latin Bloc Studies Military Action," and Lydia Chavez, "Guatemala's Interest in Regional Pact Wanes," *New York Times* (November 11, 1983), pp. A1, 10; (November 23, 1983), p. A14.

40. Joseph B. Treaster, "Caribbean War Games: Not Everyone Is Delighted," *New York Times* (September 16, 1985), p. A2.

41. Lou Cannon and Don Oberdorfer, "$20 Million U.S. Aid Given to Honduras," and Sam Dillon and Tim Golden, "Honduran Says U.S. Exaggerated Danger of Nicaraguan Raid," *Washington Post* (March 26, 1986), pp. A1, 12 (April 3, 1986).

42. Allistar Sparks, "Nonaligned 99 Convene; U.S. Policies Targeted," *Washington Post* (September 2, 1986), p. A12.

43. John M. Goshko, "U.S. and Israelis Expand Political Ties," *Washington Post* (November 30, 1983), pp. A1, 10.

44. Ann Devoy, "Reagan Commits to Israel," *USA Today* (November 23, 1983), p. 4.

45. David B. Ottoway, "Egypt's Mood Turns Against Close U.S. Ties," *Washington Post* (January 30, 1945), p. A14.

46. U.S.-Jordanian ties have also been frustrated by bad luck. In October 1983 an American effort to create a Jordanian rapid deployment force—an Arab, local intervention capability against threats to moderate Arab governments—was destroyed by premature publicity as the administration attempted to secure quiet funding for the project from Congress.

47. David B. Ottoway, "F-15 Fighters for Saudis are on Hold," *Washington Post* (September 10, 1985), p. A6; Karen DeYoung, "British Get $4.5 Billion Plane Order," *Washington Post* (September 27, 1985), pp. A1, 32.

7

THE CONTINUING QUEST FOR COLLECTIVE DEFENSE

Alan Ned Sabrosky

The central theses of this volume can be stated directly. The world is increasingly complex; the balance of power therein is changing; and security is increasingly uncertain, even for a major power such as the United States. The ambiguity surrounding the definition and distribution of effective power in world politics certainly does not automatically imply a corresponding increase in the number of actual or potential threats to the security of the United States, of course, or to that of any other nation. It does, however, increase the complexity of the international security environment within which all countries must act. This adds to the imponderables with which any foreign policy community must deal. It also reduces the ability of any single country to manage the problems confronting it in a purely national context. Nations are not yet truly interdependent, but purely *national* solutions to national security problems may no longer be feasible in some instances.[1]

These considerations highlight the continued importance of security concerns, broadly defined, to the United States in the coming years. They also tend to underscore the continuing importance of the quest for effective collective defense to offset those concerns. International cooperation is not unknown on a wide range of issues, some of which certainly impinge on the security of the participants, but effective collective security remains an ideal whose time has not yet come.[2] The United Nations is incapable of dealing effectively with crises without the unanimous support of the major powers, and all but irrelevant if such unanimity exists except as a means of adding a gloss of legitimacy to traditional "Great Power" politics. This obviously means that neither the United Nations nor any other international organization can adjudicate serious conflicts of interest among the major powers, much less enforce a ruling against any one of them, without their prior consent—something unlikely to be given when vital interests are at stake.[3]

RETROSPECT: AMERICA'S SYSTEM OF ALLIANCES

The dubious utility of international organizations as a means of safeguarding vital national interests necessarily directs attention to a less ambitious form of international cooperation: the bilateral or multilateral alliance. Alliances are certainly a legitimate framework for the pursuit of foreign policy objectives, however uneven their record may have been in the past. Precisely how the United States has structured that framework in the post-1945 era certainly has undergone a number of changes, as Terry L. Deibel pointed out in Chapter 6. His characterization of the shift in focus of U.S. alliance commitments from one emphasizing strategic purpose in the Truman years, through an aggregation of tactical artifacts in the Eisenhower years, to informal and more indirect undertakings such as security assistance agreements in more recent years, can well be seen as a form of prudent adaptation to a changing international security environment.

Prudent or not, however, the contributors to this volume properly point out the existence of a number of serious concerns with respect to the aggregate U.S.-centered system of alliances—formal or informal, direct or indirect—in place today. Some of these concerns are generic; others seem most pronounced in NATO, America's principal alliance commitment.

Two of the principal generic considerations noted by Alan Ned Sabrosky are the ubiquity and the unreliability of alliances—American or not—in the modern world. The nature of the Soviet-American relationship negates any reasonable prospects for an alliance between equals for the foreseeable future. Yet alliances between states of markedly *un*equal power historically have been unstable and often uncomfortable (albeit in different ways) for their members. The result is a situation in which the United States today has "relatively few genuine allies, many clients, and several obvious encumbrances." (See Chapter 1 of this volume.)[4] Further, that American "overcommitment" observed by Sabrosky has not abated with the shift to informal alliances. There appears to be considerable merit to Deibel's reservations about "the stability of the Carter/Reagan commitment tier." (See Chapter 6.)

Even with the more formal alliances, the doubts expressed by Earl C. Ravenal with regard to the continued inability of extended deterrence in NATO-Europe (see Chapter 2) apply at least as forcefully to other

U.S. alliance commitments elsewhere. To be sure, these reservations may be ill-founded. But as both Karen A. McPherson and Gregory D. Foster acknowledged, "differences in perception (shaped by geo- ~hical and historical circumstances)" have given rise to these and ither "questions concerning the commitment, the intentions, and the motives of alliance partners." (See Chapters 4 and 5.) There is simply no objective basis for assuming that all members of any alliance have the same security objectives, or that what one nation does to enhance its own security necessarily has (or is seen to have) a similar impact on the interests of any of its alliance partners. Indeed, the recent American experience with the ANZUS (Australia–New Zealand–United States) Treaty is but one example of the strategic consequences of differences in national interests, goals and priorities among the membership of an alliance.

All of these issues (and others as well) are manifest in NATO. Perhaps it is still generally accepted that the so-called "old truths" of the alliance are still valid, insofar as the need for a collective response to a Soviet threat and the ultimate reliance on a nuclear deterrent of that threat are concerned.[5] At the very least, NATO has, as James P. O'Leary concluded, "attained its fundamental objective: the assurance of peace in Europe." Like many others, O'Leary also remains "guard-edly optimistic about the capabilities of the alliance membership . . . (to eschew) debilitating protectionist 'beggar-thy-neighbor' policies." (See Chapter 3.)

Nevertheless, there are still numerous questions about the innate robustness and long-term viability of NATO as an institution. Foster acknowledges that "NATO comes perilously close to fulfilling all of these criteria (for least reliable alliances)." (See Chapter 5.) Ravenal points out that to many Europeans (and to some Americans as well), "America's nuclear commitment to Europe is not so sure," (see Chapter 2) although it is not entirely clear that the Soviet Union shares those uncertainties. O'Leary wonders about the ability of those sovereign welfare states which constitute a majority in NATO to deal with a more challenging foreign policy environment "at a time when the ability of the welfare state to expand levels of productive output has become highly problematic." (See Chapter 3.) And Deibel concludes that the most recent set of commitments assumed in the post-Vietnam era have emphasized "strongpoint rather than perimeter defense," something he considers "less than ideal" for U.S. purposes and for the aggregation of power (see Chapter 6)—at least an indirect reflection of the obstacles NATO needs to overcome. Whether these problems presage the *de facto* demise of NATO, or (as McPherson has suggested) are simply manifestations "of the diverse nature of its membership" (see Chapter

4) compounded by contemporary geopolitical realities, remains to be seen.

PROSPECT: DOING BETTER

It would be fair to conclude that differences of opinion about the current status and future prospects of America's system of alliances exist. It would be equally fair, however, to acknowledge that a sound conceptual reappraisal of U.S. alliance policy is merited, if only to determine the extent to which a fundamental realignment of that policy is also in order. Good alliances and reliable allies *are* important to American security. The problem is how to ensure that the United States reaffirms good alliance commitments and dispenses with those that have become either anachronisms or encumbrances, without attempting a wholesale and politically infeasible reorientation of U.S. foreign policy in general. As Ravenal has stated, "cost and risk can be traded off, within a certain range." (See Chapter 2.) The trick is to find a set of guidelines for an alliance policy that makes strategic sense and that may be sustained politically at home and abroad, thus balancing the aforementioned cost and risk.

Perhaps the most practical course of action for the United States to adapt in this regard is a combination of selective disengagement plus reform of the existing systems of alliances. Moreover, this should be coupled with an exceedingly cautious approach to the acquisition of any new commitments abroad, formal and informal alike. Seven principles highlighted by one or more of the contributors to this volume suggest how one might pursue such a general course of action. They argue that the United States should:

• *Understand that there is a fundamental incompatibility between improved relations with the USSR and China, and the maintenance of the U.S.-centered system of alliances now in place.* For better or worse, those alliances are predicated on the existence of security threats from at least one of the principal communist powers or their proxies. Better relations (short-term or not) between the United States and either communist power undermine that perception of threat, thereby reducing the cohesion of the U.S. alliance system.

• *Avoid a preoccupation with the Soviet Union by appreciating the broader political context of contemporary global politics.* The Soviet Union does pose a challenge to some U.S. interests in some parts of the world. All challenges to U.S. interests, however, do not emanate from the USSR, and alliances cast principally in an anti-Soviet mold may be unnecessary, irrelevant, or even counterproductive if the actual threat originates elsewhere in a different set of circumstances.

• *Base U.S. alliance commitments on U.S. national interests, and not principally on the presumed existence of a so-called "moral commitment" to another nation.* Successful alliances require the existence of a community of interests among their members. The fewer the objective interests linking any two nations in an alliance, the less value it has to the stronger of them (i.e., the United States in this instance), and the greater the stridency likely to appear in both countries among those who clamor for a continuation of their alleged "special relationship."[6]

• *Focus U.S. alliance policy more on current American security requirements, and less on the perpetuation of an alliance simply because it exists.* Alliances are properly seen as instruments of foreign policy used to achieve certain objectives. They are not entities whose preservation has some intrinsic merit. Times change, and alliances should change with them; otherwise, they become entangling in the strictest sense of the term.

• *Emphasize bilateral alliances with democracies, undertaken for a period of three to five years, that would lapse automatically if not renewed by both parties at the end of that time.* Fewer is better when it comes to the management of relations within an alliance, if only because it minimizes the number of conflicting interests and points of view that need to be accommodated. It is easier for this country to justify supporting democratic regimes if they are threatened, than it is to sustain assistance to a nondemocratic state. Relatively short-term alliances with preset termination dates permit a periodic reaffirmation of useful alliances, as well as allowing alliances which have outlived their usefulness to "fade away" with a minimum of political controversy.

• *Define specific obligations for both parties to the alliance, mandating an appropriate level of reciprocity from countries which depend ultimately upon the United States for their own security.* Historically, those alliances did best which promised their members the least or required their active participation on behalf of the common good only in very carefully and narrowly defined terms. "Blank checks" given to one nation by another can be fatal to both of them. Reciprocity does not preclude competition or disagreement between allies, nor does it suggest that each signatory reaps the same advantages from an alliance. But it does acknowledge that excessive competition between alliance partners or excessive costs incurred by either of them will properly threaten the existence of the pact.

• *Encourage active alliance policies, especially in the Third World, among countries whose interests generally parallel those of the United States.* Just as all threats to U.S. interests do not originate with the

USSR, there is simply no objective need for the United States to take the lead in dealing with all problems or crises in all parts of the world. Other countries, in or out of the Third World in particular, can often do as well or better than the United States. For example, the Association of Southeast Asian Nations (ASEAN), with U.S. encouragement, is making good progress in Southeast Asia; analogues should be sought out elsewhere in lieu of direct U.S. involvement.

Adhering to these principles should allow the United States to find itself with enough good alliances that are not entangling to permit it to navigate more safely in the years ahead than would otherwise be the case. Certainly, this country would doubtless have fewer formal and informal commitments abroad than it does at present, thereby alleviating to a certain degree the overextension currently characteristic of the U.S. position in the world.

On the other hand, achieving this rationalization of American alliance policy is complicated by a number of international and domestic considerations. It is especially important, in my opinion, to keep in mind Foster's argument that "The problem (of maintaining alliance cohesion) is compounded by the fact that its underlying causes are not endemic to the United States and thus not amenable to correction by our actions alone." (See Chapter 5.) The continuing diffusion of effective power in the world, reinforced by the fragmenting effect of technology and the pervasive impact of nationalism on international affairs, can only reduce the control any one nation may have on any issue or relationship. O'Leary cautions that "long-term macrostructural trends in the global economic system . . . present a potentially more somber scenario," coupled with "a possible shift in the principal axes of world trade and investment . . . toward an Asian-Pacific axis. . . ." (See Chapter 3.) The latter in particular, to be sure, would have a double-edged impact: it would weaken one link America has with NATO Europe, but it would reinforce that same link to allies in the Pacific Basin and Far East. Finally, it is worth recalling, as Deibel put it, that "the much-discussed crises in NATO . . . are dwarfed in their scope and impact by the changes which complicate U.S.–Third World ties." (See Chapter 6.) NATO may well remain America's premier alliance, but what happens outside of Europe and Northeast Asia is increasingly likely to shape the character of America's foreign commitments.

The domestic complications arise in part from the dilemma facing any democracy in its conduct of foreign affairs, and in part from certain aspects of the American condition. Some democracies do better in foreign affairs than others, to be sure, due to differences in their constitutional order, electoral process, or foreign policy tradition. Overall, however, there is more than a measure of truth to Alexis de Tocqueville's classic judgment that "Foreign policy does not require the use of any of the good qualities peculiar to democracy but does demand the cultivation of almost all those which it lacks."[7]

In the case of the United States, the record of the post-1945 era suggests that the management of alliances, like the conduct of foreign policy in general, increasingly requires of the government and the people those attributes least evident in both.[8] As Foster remarked, the United States has "no strong foreign policy tradition," plus a "perverse pride in being quite ignorant . . . of other cultures." (See Chapter 5.) The constitutional separation of powers means that the United States simply does not "form a government," as that concept is conventionally understood, with adverse consequences in all aspects of foreign affairs.[9] The Congress in particular, as McPherson concluded, "acts, not on the basis of functional imperatives generated in the international environment, but on the basis of domestic constraints" with an eye to budgets rather than to strategy. (See Chapter 4.) Unfortunately, what is politically expedient or budgetarily prudent may not be strategically sound. There is also the consideration that what Foster called an "ingrained American aversion to war" (see Chapter 5) applies to some degree to at least one of its instrumentalities—alliances. And finally, the low level of information about foreign affairs possessed by the general public means that the so-called "brick and mortar" (public opinion) constituting the American part of the foundation of any alliance's cohesion is shaky, indeed.[10]

All of the factors surely make the formulation and execution of a viable U.S. alliance policy a formidable task. Yet, to say that a task is formidable does not mean that it is impossible. A careful reappraisal of America's alliances can and should be done pragmatically, giving proper emphasis to genuine U.S. national interests and realistic U.S. objectives in the modern world. The United States must pay greater attention to the legitimate regional interests of its allies. But those allies must also be made to recognize that their military dependence on the United States entails an obligation on their part to assist militarily—or at least to refrain from actively opposing—the United States in areas of vital concern to this country. Failure in this enterprise will mean that the future of U.S. alliances is fraught with danger rather than opportunity. Success, however, may provide that measure of unity and reciprocity that would be the hallmarks of a revitalized Western security community whose creation would contribute to a more stable international order and a more secure United States.

NOTES

The views expressed here are the author's own and do not necessarily reflect those of the U.S. Government or any of its agencies.

1. This chapter draws extensively on ideas initially developed in my "America's Choices in the Emerging World Order," *International Security Review*, 4/3 (Fall 1979); "Allies, Clients and Encumbrances," *International Security Review*, 5/2 (Summer 1980); and "Alliance Aggregation, Capability Distribution, and the Expansion of Interstate War," in A. N. Sabrosky (ed.), *Polarity and War: The Changing Structure of International Conflict* (Boulder, CO: Westview Press, 1985).

2. The distinction reflects differences in membership, obligations, and range of involvement. In principle, collective security arrangements have a larger membership, more extensive but less binding obligations, and address a wider range of issues than is the case with collective defense organizations.

3. Sabrosky, "America's Choices," p. 234.

4. A commentator on contemporary *Soviet* alliances would doubtless render a similar judgment on them.

5. Alan Ned Sabrosky, "NATO: Old Truths, New Realities," *The Retired Officer* (December 1984).

6. A careful annual review of Hans Morgenthau's classic, *Politics Among Nations* (any edition) should be required for those overseeing U.S. alliance policy.

7. Alexis de Tocqueville, *Democracy in America*, edited by J. P. Mayer and translated by George Lawrence (Garden City, NY: Doubleday and Co., 1966), esp. pp. 228–229.

8. See my "National Strategy or Coalition Strategy?" in G. Foster, *et al.* (eds.), *Planning for the Future: Towards a U.S. Grand Strategy* (New York: St. Martin's Press, forthcoming); "The War Powers Resolution: Retrospect and Prospect," in S. J. Cimbala (ed.), *The Reagan Defense Program: The First Four Years* (Wilmington, DE: Scholarly Resources, 1986); and "Political Constraints on Presidential War," in S. C. Sarkesian (ed.), *Non-Nuclear Conflicts in the Nuclear Age* (New York: Praeger, 1980).

9. Lloyd N. Cutter, "To Form a Government?" *Foreign Affairs*, 59 (Fall 1980).

10. Sabrosky, "Political Constraints on Presidential War."

ABOUT THE CONTRIBUTORS

Terry L. Deibel is professor of national security policy and associate dean of Faculty and Academic Programs, The National War College. His most recent book is *Containing the Soviet Union.*

Charles F. Doran is director of the Center for Canadian Studies and professor of international relations, School of Advanced International Studies, The Johns Hopkins University. His most recent book is *Systems in Crisis: New Imperatives for International Politics Century's End.*

Gregory D. Foster is a Virginia-based consultant who specializes in international security affairs, civil-military relations, and futures research. His most recent book is *Toward a US Grand Strategy.*

Karen A. McPherson is director of Information Services at the BDM Corporation. Her published work includes articles on defense organization and civil-military relations.

James P. O'Leary is chairman of the Department of Politics at the Catholic University of America. He has published numerous studies on international economic affairs and is completing a study of the intellectual history of political development theory.

Earl C. Ravenal, a former official in the office of the secretary of defense, is Distinguished Professor of International Relations at the Georgetown University School of Foreign Service and a Senior Fellow of the Cato Institute. Among his most recent publications is *NATO: The Tides of Discontent.*

Alan Ned Sabrosky is director of studies, Strategic Studies Institute, and holder of The General of the Army Douglas MacArthur Chair of Research at the U.S. Army War College. He is completing a study on *The Politics of Military Intervention.*

INDEX